Discover you~~r per~~ ~~S~~~~erate~~
your results.

Here's how you can start accelerating your results now: Discover your personal *CLARITY*® *Quotient* by answering 20 simple questions (multiple-choice). This quick and easy questionnaire gives you a snapshot of your current state of mind, including a stress score and an engagement score, plus suggestions for how you can improve your score quickly and easily. You can get yours for free at

www.jamiesmart.com/CQ

'*Results* is a pleasure to read and full of deep insights into preparing ourselves for a more innovative way of thinking and organizing – it provides a guiding philosophy which puts our innate capacities at the heart of everything. It is a book that anyone interested in innovation – both inside and out – should read.'

Paul Sternberg, Associate Dean and Head of Design
Innovation, Ravensbourne University

'There is a magic in this book, offering wisdom to everyone. Blink and you'll miss it. Blink and you'll get it.'

Jim Lewcock, CEO, The Specialist Works

'Jamie Smart has cracked the code for creating real results in a way that fits perfectly with who you really are.'

Rich Litvin, Founder, 4PC and co-author of
The Prosperous Coach

'As an owner of a business a key success factor for me has been to focus on discovering and working with authentic people that enable me to continually deliver results. Without doubt the clarity principles and Jamie's insights have been an exponential multiplier for me in my business and personal life.'

Chris Norton, Director, Mentor Group

'*Results* provide a refreshing approach to personal and entrepreneurial transformation, and most importantly – to achieving results!'

Vlatka Hlupic, award-winning author of *The Management Shift*

'We all know we can have our best ideas, have a clarity of insight, at unexpected times. In this book, Jamie Smart shows how we can have more moments of lucid clarity and how we can marry that clarity with a propensity to action to achieve results.'

Peter Lake, Managing Director, Aztec Aspire

'Jamie Smart's book connects the dots … so often missing … between understanding and excellent, creative actions that get results in the real world. A very stimulating book!'

Steve Chandler, author of *Time Warrior*

'If you want to know what it really takes to get results and live your life to the fullest, this book is the answer. The human pursuit of success is never the problem. It's our understanding of how life works that gets in the way of our natural capacity to create, thrive and prosper as individuals and as a society. In a clear, engaging and practical way, Jamie lays out a crucial road map that will show you how getting results is far easier than you realize. Highly recommended.'

Chantal Burns, No. 1 bestselling author of *Instant Motivation,*
www.consciousleadershipschool.com

'*Results: Think Less, Achieve More* is total wisdom power. Understanding what Jamie Smart presents will allow you the insights and realizations that awaken your innate ability to create truly transformative results.'

Mark Howard, PhD, Three Principles Institute

'*Results: Think Less, Achieve More* points you to the blueprint of where success truly comes from. This book will guide you to the source of life-changing insights. Well-done Jamie!'

Catherine Casey, M.A. Clinical Psychology,
Principle Based Consultant

'*Results* is an insightful and impactful book that flies in the face of the all too common shallow and ineffective self-help advice. This book has the potential to make a significant positive impact on your life.'

Simon Hazeldine, bestselling author of *Neuro-Sell*

'In this compelling book, Jamie Smart de-mystifies what underlies true transformation and your ability to get results in any aspect of your personal and professional life. Put on your seat belt and be prepared to have your conventional way of seeing the world be rocked, while simultaneously being introduced to an exciting new way of perceiving yourself and your world!'

Dicken Bettinger, Ed.D., retired psychologist, global seminar
leader, founder of 3 Principles Mentoring,
and co-author of *Coming Home*

'The power of a clear mind is pretty much universally understood when it comes to stillness, tranquility, and happiness. Yet almost never is it linked to achievement, excellence, and consistent results. Until now. In this profound book, Jamie Smart walks us through the extraordinary (and innate) process of experiencing a shift of consciousness or change of heart, first. Then cultivating the outcomes of our dreams becomes as simple as one, two, three.'

Garret Kramer, founder of Inner Sports and author of
Stillpower and *The Path of No Resistance*

'The simple, yet profound, principles discussed in this book reveal our true nature and with it the inherent, natural potential to relax, enjoy life, be our authentic self, find clarity and create the results we want in our personal and professional lives.'

Rita Shuford, PhD

'It's perfect for those seeking to live out their purpose, looking for motivation and inspiration and those who want to challenge themselves and better understand the interconnectedness of personal and business transformation. This book is an incredible resource allowing you to have the clarity to be the change you want to see in the world!'

Conor Houston, Programme Director, Centre for Democracy and Peace Building

'This book is an insightful, powerful and unforgettable gem. Jamie Smart gently guides the reader to experience profound insights which will forever alter their view of reality – and transform their results. A must read!'

Carl Harvey, Founder, Abundance Book Club

'Simply captivating. Well articulated and to the point. *Results* is without a doubt Jamie's finest work yet. A must read for any busy business owner who wants to accelerate their results with less effort.'

Dan Bradbury, Entrepreneur and author of *Breeding Gazelles*

'*Results* is the blueprint for a world of more love, connection and true prosperity. We often live under the misunderstanding that motivation and success should come easy, when actually it takes courage. If you are willing to take that step, this is your book.'

Virginia Salas Kastilio, Snapchat Influencer, Speaker and Strategist; CEO of Ginicanbreathe Consulting www.ginicanbreathe.com

'I have worked with the CLARITY principles personally and with my leadership team. The results we have achieved are remarkable in terms of the impact across our business, the velocity we are able to achieve these in and the engagement of our people into the leadership direction and vision. Clarity is our guiding principle as a team. Smart's new book *Results: Think Less, Achieve More* shows in a clear, easy-to-understand way what we've discovered through our own experience: that clarity plus action equals results!'

Murray Pearce, Managing Director, Infinigate UK

RESULTS

Think Less. Achieve More.

Jamie Smart

Library of Congress Cataloging-in-Publication Data

Names: Smart, Jamie (Business consultant), author.
Title: Results : think less, achieve more / Jamie Smart.
Description: Hoboken : Capstone, 2016. | Includes index.
Identifiers: LCCN 2016022151| ISBN 9780857087096 (paperback) | ISBN
    9780857087133)(Adobe PDF) | ISBN 9780857087126 (epub)
Subjects: LCSH: Insight. | Thought and thinking. | Decision making.
Classification: LCC BF449.5 .S637 2016 | DDC 158–dc23 LC record available at
https://lccn.loc.gov/2016022151

A catalogue record for this book is available from the British Library.

ISBN 978-0-857-08709-6 (pbk)
ISBN 978-0-857-08713-3 (ebk) ISBN 978-0-857-08712-6 (ebk)

10 9 8 7 6 5 4 3 2 1

Cover design: Wiley

Set in 10/13 SabonLTStd by Aptara Inc., New Delhi, India
Printed in Great Britain by TJ International Ltd, Padstow, Cornwall, UK

To Team Clarity

Contents

Foreword

....

The first thing you need to know about Jamie Smart is this: He's nuts.

I'm not talking about the '*locked in a padded cell, claiming to be Napoleon*' kind of nuts. I'm talking about something much more dangerous; the '*here's to the crazy ones*' kind of nuts. The '*willing to be true to yourself and do whatever it takes, no matter what the cost*' kind of nuts. The kind that sets out to do the impossible and transforms how you see the world in the process. The totally lovable kind of nuts.

I first met Jamie in 2006, shortly after I sold my digital startup to BSkyB. In the course of the conversation, he asked me if I'd mentor him on growing his business. I refused, not because I didn't want to, but because I simply didn't have the time, but the second thing you need to know about Jamie is this: He's persistent. *Extremely* persistent. He kept asking and I kept refusing over the course of several weeks until finally, we made a deal: I would mentor him, but if we agreed something was the right thing for him to do, and he *didn't* do it, I would fire him as a client.

I expected this arrangement only to last a few weeks, but it's now 10 years later, and I still haven't fired him. Instead, he's become a dear friend, and we've each grown in ways that neither of us could have anticipated. Both of us have walked away from 'sure thing' ventures to follow our hearts. I left Smarta, the company I founded and grew through the midst of the recession. Jamie left the field he was a leader in and headed in the opposite direction to explore the principles behind clarity of mind and high-performance. And that's the third thing about Jamie: He's willing to follow the truth, wherever it leads. When my first book *Stop Talking, Start Doing* got knocked off the top of the bestseller charts after 14 months at number 1, it was no surprise to me that *his* first book CLARITY was the one that took its place.

Which brings us to Jamie's latest book, RESULTS: *Think Less, Achieve More*. The reason I habitually used to refuse to coach and mentor people (and said 'no' to Jamie initially) was this: The people who asked me to coach them inevitably turned out to be unwilling or unable to take the action needed to create the results they wanted. They seemed to get paralyzed with fear of criticism, fear of failure or fear of success. They'd get stuck and make excuses, claiming they lacked that 'special something' they needed to move forward. They'd say *'I'd do it if only I had more confidence...'*.

More self-belief... Less doubt... More creativity... Less uncertainty... More courage... Less fear...

This had always puzzled and perplexed me. *I* could see people were capable of great things; why couldn't *they* see it? *I* knew that we each have the ability to create the results that matter to us; why didn't *everyone else* know it? Why is it that people so often struggle to create the results they want?

RESULTS: *Think Less, Achieve More* doesn't just *answer* this question; it takes you much further, giving you a practical solution that's both simpler and more powerful than you may ever have imagined. And the answer has never been more important. The world is in a state of constant flux, with massive uncertainty and huge opportunities. There's never been a better time to be dreaming big and taking action. Twenty years from now, people will look back on this as a 'golden age', a time when the field was wide-open and there was everything to play for.

This book is going to wake up your innate ability to create results. As you go through the three transformations that Jamie covers so masterfully, you're going to get more in touch with who you really are, and what really matters to you. As you tap in to your authentic purpose and direction, you're going to start discovering an unsuspected ability to take action and move forward, even if you can only see the next step. And, while that's great, the key to all of this is something even *more* important: discovering who you really are (I know that may sound strange, but bear with me). Most of us have spent so long trying to be who *others* have told us we should be that we've lost touch with our true selves. And this is the real genius of RESULTS. You see, your ability to get results flows *directly* from who you really are. Your *authenticity* is the source of your *power*. One of my favourite artists, Curtis Jackson (aka 50 Cent) puts it beautifully:

> 'The greatest fear people have is that of being themselves. They want to be 50 Cent or someone else. They do what everyone else does even if it doesn't fit where and who they are. But you get nowhere that way; your energy is weak and no one pays attention to you. You're running away from the one thing that you own – what makes you different. I lost that fear. And once I felt the power that I had by showing the world I didn't care about being like other people, I could never go back.'

You're going to start waking up to that same source of power and fearlessness as you read this book. And don't be too surprised if you find yourself having more fun, bigger ideas and better relationships in the process. As you get an understanding of the principles behind RESULTS, you're going to find yourself having less on your mind, and being more present to the richness of the here and now. And here and now is the best place to start creating what matters to you.

We live at a time of increasing volatility, uncertainty and complexity. We're each here for a reason, with our own unique gifts to give. It's never been more important for each one of us to wake up to who we really are, and play our part in the shaping of our lives, our communities and our world. As well as answers, we need visionaries; people who are willing to challenge what we hold to be true. And that's the other thing you need to know about Jamie: What he's about to show you may turn everything you've ever believed on its head. And it turns out that's a wonderful place to start.

Sháá Wasmund, MBE

London, 2016

Introduction

However beautiful the strategy, you should occasionally look at the results.

Sir Winston Churchill
Former UK Prime Minister, winner of the
Nobel Prize in Literature, 1953

'What's the number one result that you believe would have the biggest positive impact in your life?'

Over the years, I've asked variations on this 'number one result' question to many thousands of people during talks, workshops and one-to-one coaching sessions. And while their backgrounds are incredibly diverse, their *initial* response is remarkably similar. Invariably, people...

Stop... Go quiet... Get reflective...

Your biggest return on investment

As the responses begin to emerge, they reveal something very powerful. Your answer to this question shows what you currently *believe* would give you your biggest 'return on investment' (ROI) for the time, energy, effort and other resources it would take to achieve it. When I was first asked the question by my coach (a successful entrepreneur) in 2006, I didn't know the answer, and I felt foolish. After all, I *should* know, shouldn't I? I was working 14-hour days growing my business, but if I didn't know the answer to this, what was I spending all my time, energy and money on? This powerful, unsettling question issued a challenge:

> *Are you willing to raise your head from the daily routine of tasks, habits and distractions, and focus your energy on what matters most to you, no matter how daunting that may seem? Are you willing to shift your attention from the soothing familiarity of 'routine' to the sometimes uncomfortable adventure of 'results'?*

Results...

We all want them, yet many of us struggle to achieve them. Or we get spectacular results in *one* area of life, while failing to attain even modest success in other important areas. There are plenty of examples...

- The successful businessman who knows he needs to lose weight and get fit, but never seems to find the time.

- The manager who's passionate about becoming a consultant or executive coach, but fears stepping away from the security of a full-time job.

- The graduate who wants to find work with meaning and purpose, but doesn't know where to start.

- The holistic therapist who has a big impact on her clients, but struggles to make ends meet.

- The CEO who wants to leapfrog the competition, but can't find the right strategy.

You probably know someone who dreams of writing the book/starting the business/clearing the debts/finding the soulmate creating the lifestyle/getting the six-pack/making that first million, but never quite seems to get there. You may even *be* that person.

Five essential questions

Motivational speakers claim we can achieve whatever we want if we believe in ourselves, set clear goals and work hard. But history is littered with examples where enormous self-belief combined with clear goals and massive action yielded *little or no* satisfying results. Why? As you're going to discover, there are powerful but little-known factors that have a profound impact on your ability to create results. In fact, this book sets out to answer five essential ons:

1 What are the key factors that influence your ability to create the results you desire, and how can you develop those factors?

2 What are the obstacles that may have been holding you or your organization back from getting the results you want, and how can you avoid, eliminate or overcome those obstacles?

3   How can you increase your impact on other people, engaging them in *your* enterprises and/or empowering them to create the results *they* desire?

4   How can you leverage your true nature as a results-creator and a leader to get greater control of your livelihood, whether as a solopreneur, as an entrepreneur or by playing a bigger role in your organization?

5   How can you do all of this in a way that's healthy, natural, authentic and enjoyable?

I've spent the past 15 years helping my clients to create results that are often beyond anything they'd previously thought possible. I've worked with...

- business leaders and their teams to create inspiring visions that they've proceeded to bring into existence.

- coaches, therapists and other transformation professionals to increase their impact, grow their practices and create lifestyles they love.

- entrepreneurs to get clarity, transform their personal and professional lives and achieve breakthrough results.

- private individuals ranging from maximum-security prison inmates to chart-topping DJs; from alcoholics and drug addicts to surgeons and opera singers.

The fact that they've done it means that you can do it too. The fact that you're even *reading* this means you have an innate capacity to live a life you love and create meaningful results in the process. And I don't want you to take my word for it. Instead, as you read this book, I'll be inviting you to test my claims in your own life and against your personal experience so you can discover the truth of this for yourself. It doesn't even matter if you don't yet know what results you want to create. As you deepen your understanding of the principles we'll be exploring together, you're going to start seeing your world with new eyes, getting clarity about what you want to bring into being, and having it happen in ways you may never have anticipated until now.

Your results may be closer than you think

The first time I was asked the *number one result* question, I eventually managed to identify the thing I believed would give me the most leverage. I wanted to generate income by putting my educational products online so I could stop selling my time, and put my energy into growing my business. 'How long do you think it will take to do that?' my coach asked. I told her I thought it would take between 18 months and 3 years. This was the same answer I'd come up with when I'd first had the idea, 18 months previously. In fact, that '18 months to 3 years' timeline always seemed to be floating ahead of me, keeping my goal the same elusive distance away, like a juicy carrot dangling from a pole attached to a donkey's head. But it turned out that my estimate was wrong by several orders of magnitude; in the end, it only took six weeks. As is so often the case, it turned out that I had a lot of the pieces in place, but hadn't realized it (it's very likely that this is the case for you too). In the process, I discovered one of the most important things you can realize about creating results:

> *There's a shortest possible time required for you to create a result, but nobody knows how long that shortest possible time is. The only way to discover it is experimentally, by taking action.*

Your results may be closer than you think. Of course, we live in a material world, and there are certain universal laws or 'principles' that cannot be violated (e.g. the principle of gravity). But all too often it is not material laws, but rather our *beliefs, concepts and misunderstandings* which place artificial limits on the results we produce, on the impact we have and on our enjoyment of life in general.

The process of transformation

By early 2008, my business was running on autopilot and I was ready to celebrate with my first 'mini-retirement', a three-month holiday at a Canadian ski resort. I was delighted with what my team and I had accomplished, and I believed this trip would yield another satisfying result; a big jump in my skiing ability combined with a sense of peace, completeness and success. But I was wrong. After a brief period of euphoria, I found myself distracted and dissatisfied, with a busy mind and feeling like there was something missing. I felt stuck, so I cut my trip short and flew home without realizing I was at the very beginning of a massive transformation; a transformation that would see me…

- sell the business I'd spent so much time and energy developing,
- walk away from the field I'd become a leader in, and
- start over and move in an entirely new direction.

That was over eight years ago, and they've been some of the most exciting, fulfilling, challenging and joyful years of my life. It's been (and continues to be) a process of transformation, and that, in essence, is the purpose of this book: to guide you in the process of more and more fully embracing your *true nature* as a results-creator. For reasons of clarity and simplicity, the process is organized around three distinct transformations:

Part One – GROUNDING
Your Personal Transformation

Imagine you're building a skyscraper; the higher you want the building to go, the deeper the foundation has to be. The purpose of Part One is to help you develop your foundations: the key qualities and internal resources of a powerful results-creator. While grounding is the foundation piece, it's often the last place people look when it comes to creating outstanding results. Your grounding is what governs your ability to move forward in the face of uncertainty, and make a real difference in the world. Grounding also determines the impact you're able to have on others, whether as a business leader, a coach, a parent, a partner or a friend. This is the deep understanding of yourself and the human condition that is the basis for all powerful transformation. As you move through your personal transformation, you're going to find yourself experiencing certain *automatic and inevitable results*. You may notice that you're developing greater confidence, clarity and peace of mind. You're also likely to find yourself experiencing a reduction in stress, worry and anxiety. As you approach the end of Part One, you may start becoming aware of a greater sense of purpose, direction and leadership as you start taking action and moving forward.

Part Two – IMPACT
Your Interpersonal Transformation

As human beings, we have a more highly evolved capacity for connection and relationship than any other species on the planet. It's not only a highly effective survival strategy (it's made us the world's most deadly predators); it's also an extraordinary leverage point when it comes to creating results. The purpose of Part Two is to support you in creating connection and impact in *all* your relationships. Your interpersonal transformation will give you the confidence and ability to have a greater impact on others, secure in the knowledge that you have something of genuine value and relevance to contribute. Whether as a business leader, a transformation professional, a parent or a colleague, impact means the difference between making a difference and wasting your breath. You're going to be introduced to the *Clarity Impact Model*, the tried and tested tool used by some of the world's most impactful coaches, consultants and other transformation professionals. In this section you should start to notice certain results emerging easily as the result of your being exposed to the principles in this book. You're going to be discovering the kind of effortless relationship skills that are the essence of powerful communication, whether you're giving a presentation, selling a prospect, coaching a colleague or connecting with your loved ones. You're also going to discover the secrets to dealing with difficult people, and the unexpected keys for motivating others to make changes and take action.

Part Three – LEVERAGE
Your Commercial Transformation

Your commercial transformation is about amplifying your impact, taking control of your livelihood, and moving into a world of abundance through connection, innovation and service. Whether you're an employee in an organization, running your own business or are looking to transition from one to the other, a service-orientation combined with new-economy savvy are essential for taking control of your commercial transformation and creating the livelihood you desire. You're going to be transforming your relationship to prosperity, and taking control of your income as you awaken your inner entrepreneur (whether as a solopreneur, business owner or a star player in a larger organization). You'll be learning how to move with the disruptive forces transforming the business world, and learning how to thrive in the increasing complexity of the commercial landscape.

Subtractive psychology: Less is more

While this book is divided into three sections for practical purposes, they actually describe three different aspects of one transformation: the process of becoming the person who can create the results you're here to create, and more fully live the life you're here to live. Most approaches for creating results are *additive*, giving you theories, techniques and concepts to remember, practise and apply. While additive approaches are often compelling, they rarely yield the desired results (for reasons we'll explore later). Fortunately, the understanding you're going to be developing as you read this book is *subtractive*. Instead of giving you more to remember, the principles you're going to be learning will take things off your mind, giving you *less* to think about. As a result, you're going to have a clear mind, more of the time, and more space for the endeavours and experiences that matter.

We are living in a VUCA world

We are in a time of increasing volatility, uncertainty, complexity and ambiguity (VUCA). Silicon Valley startups are disrupting entire industries. Airbnb was recently valued at $25 billion (November 2015), making it more valuable than the Hyatt Hotels Corporation or the InterContinental Hotels Group (owner of Holiday Inn and Crowne Plaza). This despite the fact that Airbnb has a fraction of the number of employees and owns *no hotels*. Uber continues to dominate the taxi trade in many of the world's largest cities, and book-lovers are using bookshops as unofficial 'Amazon showrooms', browsing the books on display then ordering the ones they want on their smartphones or downloading them to their Kindles. While no-one knows what the future will bring to these companies and these industries, one thing is clear; the world is changing fast and it's unlikely to slow down anytime soon. These turbulent times bring both risk and opportunity. The purpose of this book is to help you mitigate the risks and make the most of the opportunities while enjoying your life to the full.

At the end of each chapter you'll find...

- **Bottom line results**, a concise summary highlighting how this chapter applies in the business/commercial context.

- A **Practicality check** to connect your discoveries from the chapter to the results you want to create.

- An **Experiment** that will only take you a few minutes and will help you further embed what you're learning and generate new insights.

- A **web link** you can use to share your insights, connect with others and access videos and other additional learning materials.

The ultimate leverage point

This introduction started with the *number one result* question. As you've read, my *first* answer to this question initiated a chain of events that resulted in me sitting on the side of a ski slope, with sore feet and a troubled mind. But the subsequent transformation revealed a far more powerful answer to the question: a *new* leverage point that proved to be the key to creating the results that really matter to you and for you, and enjoying your relationships and your life more and more fully. In Part One of this book, you're going to be introduced to what I consider to be the *ultimate* leverage point…

Bottom line results: To grow your business results in a way that's healthy, fulfilling and sustainable, you and your team need to grow as individuals. The three transformations you'll be going through as you read this book represent the *ultimate leverage point* for your personal evolution; a framework for you to maximize the return on your investment of time, energy, money and other resources as you create the results that *truly* matter to you in a way that fits with your true nature.

keep exploring ⁖ connect with others
share your discoveries ⁖ deepen your understanding

Experiment: What's the number one result that – if you were to achieve it – you believe would have the biggest positive impact in your life? Ask yourself this question, or get someone else to ask you. You may come up with a number of different answers before settling on one that 'feels right'. Of course, your answer to this question is likely to change and evolve as you continue reading this book. It can be fun and interesting to make a note of what your answer is now, then compare it to the answer you give when you reach the end of the book (I'll ask the question again when we get there).

www.jamiesmart.com/resultsintro

PART ONE

GROUNDING
Your Personal
Transformation

Without self knowledge, without understanding the working and functions of his machine, man cannot be free, he cannot govern himself and he will always remain a slave.

George Gurdjieff
Philosopher, composer, teacher

The brain can only assume its proper behaviour when consciousness is doing what it is designed for: not writhing and whirling to get out of present experience, but being effortlessly aware of it.

Alan Watts
Philosopher, author, speaker

1

You're Built for Reality; You're Optimized for Results

You are braver than you believe, stronger than you seem, and smarter than you think.

A.A. Milne
Novelist, poet, creator of Winnie-the-Pooh

'This system uses your innate capacities and instinctive abilities, developed by evolution over hundreds of thousand of years...'

I'd never thought of myself as a fighter, but just a few hours into the experiment, I was hit by a sudden realization about our nature as human beings...

You're built for reality.
You're optimized for results.
You've evolved to survive, transform and thrive.

The experiment was *Krav Maga*, a powerful self-defence system invented in the 1930s to help Czech Jews protect themselves against Nazi thugs. I was doing a weekend workshop designed to train ordinary people to respond quickly and effectively in dangerous situations. And why is it so effective? Because it runs on the 'operating system' of your *innate capacities and instincts*; pre-existing abilities that show up *automatically*, without you having to think about it consciously. I'd never thought of myself as a fighter, but in just a few hours I was introduced to the fighter that had been right there within me, my whole life.

You're going to be introduced to the 'operating system' of your *innate capacities and instincts* for creating meaningful results and living a life you love. As you discover the results-creator that's been *right there within you* your whole life, your ability to create the results you desire and enjoy the process is going to increase exponentially.

You're built for reality, optimized for success, with the factory-settings for creating results. By definition... Whether you believe it or not. There's a built-in quality check that nature has performed on every one of your ancestors going back millions of years: were they fit enough, resilient enough, attractive enough, creative enough, aware enough, courageous enough and wise enough to get safely to breeding age, have children and pass on their genetic material? The fact that you're here means the answer to that question was 'yes', hundreds of thousands of times in succession.

You are a state-of-the-art results-creator, tempered in the furnace of millions of years of evolution.

This means that the hardware and software that comprises you have been through countless iterations, beautifully tuned, improved and adjusted for living in this world. You're built for being, walking, talking, loving, learning, playing, working, resting, thinking, making, growing, appreciating, reflecting, realizing, transforming, creating and much more. And one of the most valuable gifts that helps you survive and thrive in reality is your innate capacity for realization and insight.

You have an innate capacity for realization and insight

A realization is a fresh new thought; an insight that brings your understanding more closely into alignment with the truth of some aspect of life. History has numerous examples of dramatic realizations that have changed the world, for instance...

- Isaac Newton's insights into the principle of gravity that transformed our understanding of the material world and paved the way for the Industrial Revolution.

- The realizations about 'invisible matter' on doctors' hands that prompted Ignaz Semmelweis' pioneering of antiseptic procedures.

- James Watson's breakthrough discovery of DNA's double-helix structure, leading to numerous modern-day applications including agriculture, pharmaceuticals and forensics.

Realizations reveal pre-existing facts about the reality you're built for

In each case, the realization revealed the existence of *pre-existing facts* about some aspect of life; principles or laws behind how life *already* works. There are many more examples that make the history books, but it may surprise you to learn that you've had countless realizations and insights in *your own life…*

Let's start with a universal example: walking. You spent the months before you were born in a near-weightless environment. Then you emerged into this world and started learning about the implications of *gravity*; a pre-existing fact of life. As you started exploring this new domain, you effortlessly processed the megabytes of data pouring through your senses and had realizations about the *fact* of gravity. These realizations came *automatically*, without you even having to think about it consciously. By the time you were able to stand on two feet and walk freely, your realizations had given you a deep 'embodied understanding' of the implications of gravity. Today, your ability to walk is built on that embodied understanding; an understanding you developed *without even knowing you were doing it.*

You have an innate capacity for realization.
A realization brings you more closely into
alignment with reality.
The more aligned with reality you are, the more
effective you can be at creating results.

Realizations give rise to results

Look around you… How many of the things that you can see have been created by human beings? Each one of these objects exists because someone, somewhere had a realization; a 'lightbulb moment'. Your mobile phone (for instance) exists as the result of countless realizations, insights and discoveries. They may have started with Alexander Graham Bell's invention of the telephone in the 1870s, but numerous other people's realizations and results have combined to bring you the device you now use. Think about it:

- The designer who envisioned the model you own

- The people who created the apps that run on it

- The musician who composed the ringtone you hear

- etc

Every one of these 'links in the chain' represents a cascade of insights and realizations that have given rise to results.

Realization is a natural function of your mind

You've had countless realizations and insights over the years; 'hits' of fresh new thinking that have aligned your embodied understanding of life more closely with reality. If you'd like a simple metaphor for this, look at the FedEx logo. There are two images, hiding in plain sight, contained within the logo: A white spoon (poetically concealed in the word 'Fed') and a white arrow (hidden in the word 'Ex'). These two images have always been part of the 'reality' of the logo. You may have looked at them hundreds or even thousands of times. You may not have *noticed* them until now, but they've always been there. The mechanism that takes you from 'looking' to 'seeing' is *realization*; a hit of fresh new perception that arrives from *beyond* your existing model of reality. And once you've seen them, you'll never be able to un-see them. Your realization will have brought your understanding more closely into alignment with reality. Every time you see the FedEx logo from now on, you're going to be reminded of your built-in capacity for realization, of the principles we're exploring in this book, and your innate ability to *get results*.

Figure 1.1: The FedEx logo

You possess superpowers

Your innate capacity for realization is one of a number of 'superpowers' you possess; the *deep drivers* you benefited from as you learned to walk. Take a moment to imagine you're looking out at the world through the eyes of a toddler...

- Your innate capacity for **direction** shows you a purpose and possibility that inspire and motivate you.

- Your innate capacity for **resilience** enables you to take risks, recover and get back up every time you fall over.

- Your innate capacity for **creativity** has you innovating different approaches and creating solutions to problems.

- Your innate capacity for **authenticity** means you trust yourself and stay true to your authentic desires.

- Your innate capacity for **intuition** lets you know when to practise, when to rest and when to try something different.

- Your innate capacity for **presence** keeps you close to reality; aware, insightful and learning rapidly.

- Your innate capacity for **connection** allows you to be playful and loving, secure in yourself and your world.

- Your innate capacity for **clarity** lets you play full-out, clear-minded and at the very edge of your abilities.

Practicality check: How is realizing I'm built for reality going to help me get results?

These *deep drivers* are the 'default settings' of your nature as a results-creator. As a small child, you threw yourself fully into your passions and enthusiasms, without hesitation, fear of criticism or the concept of failure. You had full access to these deep drivers, and took action to create the results you envisioned. Those deep drivers are still there within you, ready to serve you in creating the results you desire and a life you love. For the remainder of this book, we're going to be using the term 'clarity' as a shorthand for the innate capacity for results-creation and rich experience of life you were born with. Putting it simply, *Clarity plus Action equals Results...*

CLARITY   plus   **ACTION**   equals   **RESULTS**

Figure 1.2:   The CLARITY® Results Model

You can remember this easily by using the acronym and metaphor 'CAR' (Clarity + Action = Results). As a driver, the more deeply you understand the principles of motoring, the more flexibly, skillfully and enjoyably you're able to use a car to get you where you want to go. Similarly, the more deeply you understand the principles we're going to be exploring in this book, the more flexibly, creatively and enjoyably you're going to be able to create the experiences and results you want in your life.

Whatever your experience has been so far in life, you have good reason to be hopeful. You have these innate capacities and deep drivers within you. As you get a deeper understanding of the principles behind clarity, you're going to find these capacities and instincts showing up automatically, more and more of the time, without you having to think about it consciously.

So if we all have these innate capacities and instincts, what gets in the way? If we're all state-of-the-art results-creators, why is it so often a struggle to solve our problems or make changes? Why does it sometimes seem so challenging to get results?

Bottom line results: The fact that you're alive means you're a state-of-the-art results-creator, optimized by millions of years of evolution. As the rate of change continues increasing, the ability to sense and respond to threats and opportunities is becoming increasingly important. You possess innate capacities that are the *deep drivers* of business success. Your (and your organization's) ability to sense, respond and create results is a function of your *realization* of those innate capacities.

keep exploring ⊹ *connect with others*
share your discoveries ⊹ *deepen your understanding*

Experiment: Take a moment to reflect on some of the things we often take for granted. For example: Your ability to walk, ride a bicycle or drive a car. Your ability to comprehend language; to listen, talk, read and write. What are some of your more powerful insights, realizations and embodied understandings that are already making a big difference to you and for you?

www.jamiesmart.com/results1

2

The One and Only Way Your Mind Always Works

....

When you have eliminated all which is impossible, then whatever remains, however improbable, must be the truth.

Sir Arthur Conan Doyle
Doctor, novelist, creator of Sherlock Holmes

'I need a formula for how this transformation is going to work...'

Ian Selby and I were 45 minutes into the first morning of a three-day 1:1 coaching intensive. Ian runs *Timbawood*, a specialist manufacturing business whose purpose is to restore and preserve Britain's architectural heritage. It's a successful, fast-growing company, but Ian had hired me because he felt stuck. He couldn't move forward and get to where he wanted to be in his work, his relationships and his life in general. He wanted clarity of direction and the ability to create new results. He wanted to experience more connection and less conflict in his relationships. We made a short list of the problems he wanted to solve, the changes he wanted to make and the goals he wanted to achieve as a result of our work together. But before we'd even finished our first session, he started to get anxious and told me, 'I need a *formula* for how this transformation is going to work'.

Suddenly, I felt stuck too. I didn't *have* a formula. Ian had paid a large sum of money to work with me, and I wasn't going to be able to give him what he wanted! My heart started to sink as my head filled up with worrying scenarios. I'd been temporarily deceived by a trick of the mind...

A trick of the mind

The single biggest barrier to progress – and the cause of most frustration, stuckness and suffering – is an innocent and widespread *misunderstanding* about how our minds work. This trick of the mind is validated and reinforced by the media, politicians, teachers, employers, friends, relatives, self-help books and even our own perceptual systems. By the time you've finished this chapter, you will have discovered the one and only way your mind *always* works, and the simple trick of the mind that stops people creating the results that matter to them. As you start to 'see through' this false belief, you'll be waking up to your true power as a results-creator.

Your experience is being generated from within you, right now!

The human mind has an extraordinary job to do. Millions of bits of information arrive at our senses every second. Our minds process that data, combine it with information from our memory banks and weave a coherent and stable perceptual reality that we experience as 'real'. The mind-made perceptual reality we construct seems so real to us that we rarely question its validity...

Look around at the environment you're in. Your experience of everything you can see, hear, feel, taste and smell is being generated from *within you*, moment to moment. Even the things you can see and hear 'out there' are experiences being generated from within you (albeit, with a live data-feed). It seems to us as though we look out through our eyes at a world 'out there', but our perception is less like looking through the lens of a camera and more like a projector or a set of virtual reality goggles. Please note: I'm not saying that everything 'out there' is being generated from within you; I'm saying that your *experience* of everything 'out there' is being generated from within you, using the power of THOUGHT: the reality principle.

THOUGHT: the reality principle

People think. The principle of THOUGHT refers to our innate capacity to generate a perceptual reality; an outer and inner world that we can see, hear, feel, taste and smell. This principle is also the source of the countless thoughts and perceptions that arise in the course of a day.

- You were born into the principle of THOUGHT just as you were born into the principle of gravity.

- You use the principle of THOUGHT, *automatically* and *effortlessly* to generate a coherent perceptual reality, moment to moment.

- You're always living in a THOUGHT-generated perceptual reality and experiencing it as an *actual* reality.

Reality check

'Thanks Professor', I hear you say, 'but so what? What difference does it make that I'm living in a THOUGHT-generated perceptual reality? I still get evicted if I don't pay the rent'. Here's the difference it makes:

> *Your THOUGHT-generated perceptual reality is like a pair of glasses that colours everything you see.*
> *Your feelings are giving you feedback about the <u>glasses</u> you're wearing, <u>not</u> what you're looking at.*

Don't take my word for it; check your own experience. Have you noticed how...

- When you feel irritated, it can seem like it's caused by whoever or whatever you're thinking about.

- When you feel grateful, it's easy to find things to be grateful for.

- When you feel down or low, it can appear like there are really good reasons for it.

- When you feel happy, it seems like there are really good reasons for *that*.

- When you feel stressed out, it often seems like the causes are outside you.

In fact, sometimes the very situations or people which seem annoying or frustrating on one day can seem sweet or charming the next. That's because your feelings are giving you feedback on THOUGHT taking form in the moment, *not* whatever you're thinking about.

> *Thinking and feeling are two sides of the same coin...*
> *You're <u>always</u> living in the feeling of THOUGHT in the moment...*
> *But it often <u>seems</u> like you're feeling something <u>other than</u> THOUGHT.*

Moving from La-la Land to reality

This is the illusion that had me fooled when Ian said he needed a formula. Fortunately, I woke up to the fact that my feelings of anxiety and stuckness *weren't* telling me about my client, my abilities or my lack of a formula… My feelings were alerting me to the principle of THOUGHT taking an anxious form in the moment. The second I realized this, I fell out of the 'la-la land' of my cluttered thinking and back into the present; back into the reality we're built for, where the solution suddenly came to me. I wrote on the whiteboard:

$$\text{You} + \text{Misunderstanding} = \text{Stuck}$$

I said, 'Your sense of being stuck is the result of a fundamental misunderstanding of where your experience is coming from. But your innate capacity for realization will help you see through that misunderstanding and wake up to a rich, fulfilling experience of life'.

Earlier in the session, Ian had told me that when he was a young man, he was very happy-go-lucky, spontaneous and carefree. As he grew older, he had become more serious and busy-minded. He longed for the sense of freedom, fun and happiness that he used to enjoy. I told him he was going to *love* the second part of the formula:

$$\text{You} - \text{Misunderstanding} = \begin{array}{l}\text{Clarity, Freedom, Fun,} \\ \text{Spontaneity, Fulfilment,} \\ \text{Love, Happiness, Results}\end{array}$$

'Great', Ian said. 'We've got the formula we need. Let's go'.

The terrible price of misunderstanding

The 20th President of the United States, James A. Garfield, was shot by assassin Charles Guiteau on 2 July 1881. Though the bullets missed his vital organs, one became lodged deep within the president's abdomen. If nature had been left to run its course, Garfield would likely have survived the gunshots. But the president was quickly attended by doctors who, in an attempt to dislodge the bullet, inserted their unsterilized fingers and instruments into his open wound.

The president's doctors had a *fundamental misunderstanding* about the nature of infection...

By the time Garfield was shot, the British physician Joseph Lister had been pioneering antiseptic surgical procedures for 14 years. The mortality rate among his patients had dropped dramatically, and many European doctors had adopted Lister's ideas. But most American doctors of the day did not believe that germs (invisible to the naked eye) were the cause of infection. They preferred explanations they could more easily understand, and that were in keeping with the prevailing orthodoxy... the mistaken belief that an infection could have a *variety* of causes, ranging from 'miasmas' (bad air) to moral factors.

Doctors + Misunderstanding = Accidental Infection

James A. Garfield died 11 weeks later, his body riddled with infection that was the consequence of his doctors' misunderstanding.

Think about it... *The President of the United States...* He had access to his country's top doctors, but those doctors were in thrall to a fundamental misunderstanding... an illusion... a trick of the mind. History has numerous examples of this kind of illusion:

Misunderstanding/Illusion/Trick of the mind/La-la Land	The reality you're built for/ Fact of life/Pre-existing truth
Flat earth	Spherical earth
Geocentric universe (earth is the unmoving centre)	Solar system (earth goes round the sun)
Stars and planets are held in place by crystal spheres	The principle of gravity
Infection is caused by miasmas, humours, moral character and other factors	Infection is caused by germs

Once again, you're a born results-creator. The primary obstacle to you creating the results that matter to you is the outside-in misunderstanding; the mistaken belief that you're feeling something *other than* THOUGHT in the moment. As you realize this for yourself, you'll start experiencing the unexpected yet inevitable results of living more closely in alignment with the reality you're built for.

Misunderstanding/Illusion/Trick of the mind/La-la Land	The reality you're built for/ Fact of life/Pre-existing truth
The outside-in misunderstanding: it honestly seems like your feelings are giving you feedback about something *other than* THOUGHT in the moment, for example...	*The inside-out reality:* your feelings are giving you feedback about THOUGHT in the moment and *nothing else*
– Past events – Future possibilities – Current circumstances – Other people – Your skills, abilities and potentials – What you're like as a person	

Reality check

'I've seen the words "feeling" and "feelings" 10 times already in this chapter. Is this a book about emotions?' No. The sentence 'You're living in the feeling of the principle of THOUGHT taking form in the moment' can be stated in a variety of ways...

- You're living in the *experience* of THOUGHT in the moment.
- You're living in a THOUGHT-generated perceptual reality.
- You're living in your moment-to-moment state of mind/attitude/ mindset/mood.

Your whole experience of life is a THOUGHT-generated totality; an undivided unity springing into being, moment by moment. There is no division between thinking and feeling, psychology and emotion. It is *one unified experience* being created using the power of THOUGHT.

Is this emotional intelligence?

The past 20 years have seen increasing interest in 'emotional intelligence' as an explanation for high performance in certain domains (e.g. leadership, negotiation, influence). Unfortunately, attempts to add the 'skills' of emotional intelligence to people's repertoire have often achieved only patchy results until now. Why? Because emotional intelligence isn't *additive*; it's an expression of *innate capacities* that you already possess. The 'skills' of emotional intelligence emerge *naturally* when there's nothing getting in the way. And what gets in the way? Contaminated thinking arising from the outside-in misunderstanding. But as you *subtract* that misunderstanding, you're going to find the qualities of emotional intelligence emerging and developing *automatically* as you interact with others.

The power of subtraction

Over the next three days, I guided Ian through the discoveries we're going to be exploring together in this book. As he started to 'see through' the outside-in misunderstanding, he began to relax into his true nature, and wake up to the beauty of life. On the third day, we reviewed the list of outcomes Ian had made at the beginning, and he started laughing. As we went through his list of objectives, we found that each of the problems, changes and desired results looked profoundly different.

Problems	Changes	Desired results
The problem no longer existed, or...	The change no longer seemed important, or...	The result no longer seemed important, or...
The solution was now obvious, and he felt capable and motivated to resolve the problem, or...	The change had already happened, or...	The result had been replaced by something much more inspiring and natural for him, or...
The urgency was gone, and he felt comfortable and confident that the solution would emerge in due course	The urgency was gone, and he was happy to let it emerge in an organic way	The way forward was obvious, and he felt ready and excited to start creating it

I love this part of the transformation process. As you fall out of the La-la Land of your misunderstanding, you come to rest in the reality of clarity, freedom and possibility. As you start waking up to your true nature, you realize just how much power you have to live a life that deeply inspires you.

In the time since our three days together, Ian's life and business have continued to transform. As well as a new sense of energy of personal direction, he's enjoying deeper-than-ever connections in his relationships, and more fun and spontaneity in general. As Ian has introduced this understanding into his business, it's had a dramatic effect on his team and their performance. In the 24 months since Ian's intensive, his business has gone from being 'stuck' to experiencing an impressive 60% growth. He told me, 'It's wonderful to see my team flourish, take on more responsibility and be so much more productive. We're connected, aligned and all pulling in the same direction. For me personally, this shows up in my life as working less for more results.' Very importantly, he no longer feels stuck, and is enjoying sharing his newfound clarity with clients, colleagues and loved ones. And the formula I came up with for Ian ended up being boiled down to *The Clarity Equation…*

| CLARITY | equals | **CAPACITY** | minus | **CONTAMINATION** |

Figure 2.1:   The CLARITY® Equation

Practicality check: How is a deeper understanding of my mind going to help me get results?

This simple formula, *Clarity equals Capacity minus Contamination*, points us back to the innate capacities and deep drivers we talked about in Chapter 1…

- **Capacity**: You have an innate capacity for wellbeing, realization, resilience and high performance. You're built for reality and optimized for results.

- **Contamination**: The only thing that ever obscures this capacity is contaminated thinking, arising from the outside-in misunderstanding.

- **Clarity**: As you wake up from that misunderstanding and get more closely aligned with reality, clarity emerges.

As you experience greater clarity in your life, you're going to have realizations and insights into what results matter to you and for you. You'll also have greater access to your innate capacities for bringing those results into being while enjoying the process.

As you get greater clarity, you'll find problems dissolving, solutions emerging and new desires being awakened. As you start to see a bigger picture of what's possible for you, you'll be getting opportunities to let go of some excess baggage...

Bottom line results: High performance is a strong predictor of business success. A clear mind is *essential* for high performance, yet we're living at a time when our mental clarity is under attack from smartphones, social media and spam. But here's the thing: your mood is like a pair of glasses; your feelings are telling you about the glasses you're wearing, *not* what you're looking at. Seeing through the outside-in misunderstanding is the quickest, most effective way to enjoy a clear mind, more of the time, with high levels of connection, motivation and performance.

keep exploring* ⁝ *connect with others
share your discoveries* ⁝ *deepen your understanding

Experiment: What are some of your more impactful and liberating realizations and insights so far in your life? What are some of the examples you can identify where your innate capacity for realization has brought you more closely into alignment with reality? Take a few moments to reflect on the fact that this power for realization is one of the most valuable gifts you possess, even if you haven't recognized it until now.

www.jamiesmart.com/results2

3

Eliminating Worry, Anxiety and Fear of Criticism

···

The less you fear, the more power you will have.

Curtis Jackson (aka 50 Cent)
Musician, entrepreneur, actor, producer

'It's as though a lifetime of limiting beliefs and negative ideas about myself have just fallen away...'

Donna Churchman had been terrified of public speaking for as long as she could remember. Despite being extremely accomplished (Donna's an award-winning designer), she wasn't able to express herself well in large groups. She felt extreme anxiety and she worried about saying the wrong thing or looking stupid. I wasn't aware of this when I met Donna on the first weekend of my coach training programme. She was quiet through the first day. Then, partway through the morning of the second day, Donna had an earth-shaking insight. When I asked her what had happened, she told me, 'It's as though a lifetime of limiting beliefs and negative ideas about myself have just fallen away'. She'd had a sudden realization and seen through the illusion of her extreme worry and anxiety.

Worry, anxiety and fear of criticism are 'optical illusions of the mind', with no more reality than a daydream or a highway mirage. By the time you've finished this chapter, you're going to start seeing these phantoms for what they are, and further harness your ability to create results.

So what do I mean by 'optical illusions of the mind'?

The teddy bear factor

Let's take a universal example: the teddy bear. Small children are often given a stuffed toy or security blanket that they take to bed at night. If the child 'bonds' with the teddy bear, then (before long) it seems to the child like the bear is a source of peace, comfort and security. But this is a trick of the mind – 100% of the feelings of peace, security and comfort are generated from within the child. It *seems* like they're coming from the teddy bear, but the bear is neutral. If the teddy gets lost, or left behind when the family goes on holiday, it seems to the child like the *absence* of the bear is the source of their feelings of worry, anxiety and insecurity. But this *too* is a trick of the mind. The feelings may *seem like* they're coming from the *lack* of the teddy bear, but 100% of them are coming from within the child.

This example is uncontroversial, but how quickly do we change our tune when we substitute the 'adult teddy bears' of money, jobs or romantic partners? Of our future hopes, fears or uncertainties? Of our past victories, defeats or indiscretions? How different does it seem when we ponder the 'teddy bear' of our physical body, our health or our personality? 100% of your feelings of worry, anxiety and insecurity are generated from within you, even when it *seems like* they're coming from an 'adult teddy bear'. The same goes for your feelings of peace, security and comfort. The teddy bear is always neutral.

It appears as though the sun rises, but it's an illusion caused by the rotation of the earth. It seems like our feelings of security come from our income, our relationships or our teddy bears, but it's an illusion caused by our conditioning and perception. Of course, this doesn't just apply to our feelings of security; it also holds true for feelings of *insecurity*. Remember the trick of the mind from Chapter 2? Now we can expand on it...

Misunderstanding/Illusion/ Trick of the mind/La-la Land	The reality you're built for/ Fact of life/Pre-existing truth
The outside-in misunderstanding: It honestly *seems* like your feelings are giving you feedback about something *other than* THOUGHT in the moment, for example...	*The inside-out reality:* Your feelings are giving you feedback about THOUGHT in the moment and *nothing else*. 100% of your feelings are an experience of 100% of your THOUGHT-generated perceptual reality. 0% of your feelings are an experience of anything *other than* THOUGHT in the moment
– Some future event or outcome (worry and anxiety tends to be future-oriented)	
– What you're like as a person (self-doubt, shame, shyness tend to be self-oriented)	
– Past occurrences (guilt, regret, remorse tend to be past-oriented)	
– Other people (resentment, envy, jealousy tend to be other-oriented)	

The *illusion* that tricks us into believing our felt experience is being generated from something *other than* THOUGHT is both compelling and *invisible*. We all get fooled by it, and we will continue to get fooled by it from time to time. There's no immunity from this trick of the mind. There is, however, an inoculation…

> *As you continue to deepen your understanding of the*
> *principles behind clarity, you'll be tricked less often and*
> *wake up more quickly when you <u>do</u> get tricked.*

Why feelings of worry or anxiety are not the problem

Everyone sometimes experiences feelings of insecurity, such as worry, anxiety or self-doubt. That's not a problem. Those feelings are giving you feedback on the *totality* of your THOUGHT-generated experience in the moment, and that's really *useful*. The problem is that you sometimes believe your feelings are letting you know about something *other than* THOUGHT. And why is that a problem?

Here's a simple analogy: Cars have a fuel gauge and a speedometer. These are feedback mechanisms, each designed to measure *one thing*. The fuel gauge gives feedback on the amount of fuel in the car's fuel tank. The speedometer gives feedback on the speed the wheels are turning at. The fuel gauge is an expert on the fuel level *and nothing else*. The speedometer is an expert on the speed *and nothing else*. The fuel gauge doesn't know *anything* about the speed, and the speedometer doesn't know *anything* about the fuel level.

The Fuel Gauge
Gives feedback on one thing: the amount of fuel in the car's fuel tank.

The Speedometer
Gives feedback on one thing: the speed the car's wheels are turning at.

The Feeling Gauge
Gives feedback on one thing: a person's THOUGHT-generated perceptual reality in the moment.

Figure 3.1: The Feeling Gauge

Each gauge is a mechanism that gives feedback on *one thing*. If you mistakenly believed that the speedometer was giving you feedback on the fuel level, you would soon be in trouble.

Why feelings are nothing personal

Your feelings are an incredibly precise and accurate gauge or signal. They've evolved over hundreds of thousands of years, to help you live, thrive and survive here on earth (remember, you're built for reality). Your body has countless feedback loops and signalling systems to govern things as diverse as body temperature, hydration and pH level. Just as your car's gauges give you precise feedback about fuel level and speed respectively, your internal 'gauges' each give you feedback on one thing:

> *Your feelings are a feedback mechanism, designed to*
> *measure one thing.*
> *Your feelings give you feedback on the principle of*
> THOUGHT *taking form in the moment.*
> *Your feelings are a reflection of* THOUGHT *in the moment*
> *and nothing else.*

Feelings are *impersonal*. Our feelings don't know anything about our past, our future, our circumstances, other people or what we're like. Our feelings are a mechanism that give feedback on *one thing*: the totality of our THOUGHT-generated perceptual reality in this moment. When we mistakenly believe our feelings are letting us know about something *other than* that, we've slipped into La-la Land.

We sometimes believe we're in La-la Land

'La-la Land' is a nickname for a world that people believe in, but that doesn't actually exist. Here are some examples of historical or fictional La-la Lands people have believed in:

Literary La-la Lands	Scientific La-la Lands
Narnia (C.S. Lewis)	Flat earth with a dome (Babylonian)
Wonderland (Lewis Carroll)	Crystal spheres (Aristotelian)
Middle Earth (J.R.R. Tolkien)	Geocentric model (astronomy before Copernicus, Galileo and Kepler)
Land of Oz (L. Frank Baum)	
Discworld (Terry Pratchett)	Phlogiston theory (chemistry before Lavoisier)
	Miasmas and atmospheres (medicine before germ theory)

When we believe in a La-la Land, we're believing the world works in a way that is not based in reality. We've slipped into misunderstanding and contaminated thinking. And here's the thing:

You're not built for a non-existent La-la Land…
You're built for reality.

The fact that you understand the reality of germs means you wash your hands regularly, cover your mouth when you cough and observe the three-second-rule if you drop a sandwich on the floor. These behaviours are grounded in a better understanding of reality than people who lived 200 years ago had. As a result of having a better understanding of *how life already works,* you get to prosper, thrive and be healthy. You're not caught up in the superstitions about illness and disease that contaminated the perceptions of people who lived 200 years ago. Your understanding is aligned more closely with the reality you're built for.

When you're 'hanging out in reality', you do very well. You get intuitions about what to do, about when to rest and when to take action. Your innate capacities are fully available to you when you're hanging out in reality, living in the present moment. You have a natural capacity to connect with other people. You have a natural capacity for insight and realization. You have a natural capacity to take action on things that matter to you. All of that and more is available to you when you're hanging out in reality. But it's a little harder to come by when you're hanging out in La-la Land. The moment a person believes that they're feeling something other than THOUGHT in the moment, they've stepped into an illusory non-reality; a world that doesn't exist.

Our instincts, our intuitions, our natural capacities… they just don't work quite as well when we believe we're hanging out in a world that doesn't actually exist. It's tough to get results there! In fact, when we believe we're hanging out in an outside-in La-la Land, our natural capacities get utilized to wake us up to reality. But here's the best bit. You *already* live in reality and you always have done. The outside-in non-reality is a dream, an illusion, a fantasy world. The only place La-la Land exists is in our heads. In reality, all is well, and you have everything you need to respond powerfully in the moment.

Once again:

> *Feelings are giving you <u>essential</u> feedback about* THOUGHT *in the moment; the glasses you're wearing…*
> *That's not a problem. The problem is that we sometimes believe our feelings are letting us know about something <u>other than</u> the glasses we're wearing…*

So let's dispense with these illusions, one by one…

Trick of the mind	Misunderstanding/ Illusion/La-la Land	The reality you're built for/Fact of life/ Pre-existing truth
	The outside-in Illusion: It seems as if a person's feelings are giving them feedback about…	*The inside-out reality:* Your feelings are giving you feedback about THOUGHT in the moment and *nothing else*

100% of your feelings are a reflection of 100% of your THOUGHT-generated perceptual reality. 0% of your feelings are a reflection of anything *other than* THOUGHT in the moment |
Worry	a future event or outcome	
Anxiety	a circumstance, past, current or future	
Self-doubt	themselves; their capabilities, their qualities, their value as a person	
Boredom	whatever's going on at the moment	
Stress	external circumstances and their ability to deal with them	
Depression	themselves, their levels of OK-ness, their life, their past and their future	
Pressure	what's expected of them/what's being asked of them	
Resentment	the past behaviour of other people	
Impatience	something they don't believe is happening fast enough	
Urgency	something they believe needs to happen quickly	
Overwhelm	the number of things/events they're thinking about	
Fraud/ Impostor syndrome	their (lack of) value or worthiness as a person	
Low self-esteem	their (lack of) value or worthiness as a person	
Social anxiety	other people, their opinion of people and their ability to interact with those people	
Fear of failure	the consequences of things not turning out in a certain way in the future	
Performance anxiety	their ability to deliver, and other people's opinion of/response to them	
Fear of public speaking	their ability to deliver, and other people's opinion of/response to them	
Fear of criticism	another person's opinion of them or their efforts	

Reality check

'Wait a minute. I've read that depression is caused by chemical and hormonal imbalances, and that neuroscientists have identified a "happiness gene". Are you really saying that stress, anxiety and depression are just a person's thinking? That the "biomedical model" of mental disorders is wrong?'

Yes and no...

Consider someone who blushes in embarrassment as a colleague tells a group of co-workers a suggestive joke. Blushing is the end result of a variety of involuntary processes. These involve neurological activity, stress hormones, neurochemicals, blood vessel dilation etc. And what causes all of this?

THOUGHT in the moment...

Their non-blushing colleagues are having a different THOUGHT-generated experience, so they don't blush.

Think about it: If something as simple as 'embarrassed thinking' can have such a profound impact on a person's brain and body (i.e. blushing), what do you think the impact of months or years of 'depressed thinking' will have had on a person's brain chemistry?

While it's possible that differences in brain chemistry and genetics have an influence on a person's state of mind, we won't be able to determine the relationship *definitively* until research is conducted by scientists who have an understanding of the nature of THOUGHT. Until that point, it's likely that 'symptoms' and 'correlations' will continue to be misinterpreted as 'causes'.

In fact, a 2013 paper by Brett J. Deacon, PhD (published in the highly regarded *Clinical Psychology Review: The Future of Evidence-Based Practice in Psychotherapy**) raises significant concerns about the biomedical model. He suggests that framing mental disorders as biochemically-induced brain diseases, then treating them with 'disease-specific' psychiatric medications has led to a lack of clinical innovation, and poor results for patients. Deacon states that 'an honest and public dialog about the validity and utility of the biomedical paradigm is urgently needed'.

*SOURCE: The biomedical model of mental disorder: A critical analysis of its validity, utility, and effects on psychotherapy research by Brett J. Deacon PhD. *Clinical Psychology Review* Volume 33, Issue 7, November 2013, Pages 846–861

When we slip into the La-la Land of the outside-in misunderstanding, we go into 'victim' mode. Our thinking accelerates and multiplies as we mistakenly attribute our feelings to external factors. But the moment we wake up to the fact of where our experience is coming from, our heads start to clear, and we fall back into the reality of the now.

Practicality check: How is eliminating worry, anxiety and fear of criticism going to help me get results?

The relationship between a clear mind and high performance is well documented. The outside-in misunderstanding is the single biggest source of the contaminated thinking that blocks people from clarity, impedes their performance and inhibits their ability to create the results that matter to them. But the CLARITY® model is ruthlessly subtractive. As you get a deeper understanding of the principles behind clarity, it's going to take things *off* your mind, and bring your innate capacities to the fore. And as clarity continues to emerge, you'll find yourself having more and more freedom to take the actions you need to create the results that matter to you.

| CLARITY | plus | ACTION | equals | RESULTS |

Figure 3.2:   The CLARITY® Results Model

Speak to 100 people like you're speaking to one person

On the day of her realization, Donna stood up and talked to the 40-person coach training group about what she'd seen. A few weeks later, she told her story in front of a Meetup group of 70 people. A few months after that, she gave an online masterclass called 'Speak to 100 people like you're speaking to one person'. These experiences awakened a passion in Donna to support her peers in the creative industry, and she now works helping creative professionals understand the principles behind clarity. In March 2015, Donna and her fellow *CLARITY®* *Coach* Ian Webster flew to Berlin and gave a presentation about these principles to 350 of the world's leading creatives at the ProMaxBDA Conference. It took courage, but Donna was surprised to discover how easy and enjoyable she found it once she realized she could express herself, free from worry, anxiety and fear.

> *As you see through the illusion of worry, anxiety and*
> *self-doubt, you open a space to create results.*

So what fills the space left by these optical illusions of the mind?

Bottom line results: Stress, worry, anxiety, frustration and fear of criticism are like sand in the gears of any organization, reducing productivity and driving counterproductive behaviour. But as you see through the trick of the mind that gives rise to them, you free yourself to give your best, set an encouraging example for others and focus on results that matter (instead of illusions that don't exist).

---

keep exploring ⁖ connect with others
share your discoveries ⁖ deepen your understanding

Experiment: A 'pizzawalk' is a simple social experiment. Here's how it works: go to the sales counter in a retail store and make an absurd request with a straight face. Examples include asking for lingerie in a butcher's shop, perfume in a toyshop or pizza in a bank. If the thought of doing a pizzawalk already has your heart pounding... where do you believe those feelings are coming from? From the future? From the request you haven't yet made? From the response of the people you're going to make the request to? Fortunately, those are all impossibilities. You're feeling THOUGHT in this moment and nothing else. Isn't that interesting? Use your common sense when you do your pizzawalks (e.g. don't make an absurd request in a restaurant where you're about to eat). Have fun! You may discover that your experience is different from how you expect it to be.

www.jamiesmart.com/results3

4

The Source of Resourcefulness, Resilience and Results

··

Most people tiptoe through life, hoping to make it safely to death.

Earl Nightingale
Author, speaker, radio personality

'I had this big epiphany the day of the earthquake...'

Mahima doesn't remember where she was when she flicked through my first book, *CLARITY*, but a phrase stuck in her mind... '100% of your feelings come from THOUGHT in the moment'. She Googled it later and started exploring the principles behind clarity. Not long after that, the massive April 2015 Nepal earthquake hit (Mahima is a crisis management consultant who lives in Kathmandu, 50 miles from the epicentre). The earthquake destroyed buildings, killing thousands, and for the first few hours, Mahima was terrified. Then she had a sudden realization:

> *Your felt experience is a reflection of THOUGHT, not your circumstances. In this moment you are as safe as you are ever going to be and as safe as you have ever been.*

As Mahima's fear evaporated, she found that she was more engaged with life, not less. She was more capable and resourceful; able to give her all to the situation, secure in the knowledge that she'd be able to handle it, whatever happened. Mahima had woken up to her inner self; her true nature.

You're capable of far more than you think you are, because you are far more than you think you are. By the time you've finished this chapter, you'll have a deeper understanding of your true nature – who you really are – the source of resourcefulness, resilience and results.

How often do you say 'I am'?

Stop for a moment, and think about some of the 'I am' concepts/constructions you use from time to time. For instance...

- I am [name]
- I am a man
- I am a woman
- I am a son
- I am a daughter
- I am a brother
- I am a sister
- I am a father
- I am a mother
- I am married
- I am free
- I am handsome
- I am beautiful
- I am ugly
- I am thin
- I am fat
- I am tall
- I am short
- I am sexy
- I am healthy
- I am single
- I am stuck

- I am clever
- I am stupid
- I am productive
- I am lazy
- I am good
- I am bad
- I am guilty
- I am innocent
- I am spontaneous
- I am bored
- I am certain
- I am peaceful
- I am worried
- I am relaxed
- I am tired
- I am energized
- I am stressed
- I am rich
- I am broke
- I am abundant
- I am poor
- I am joyful

- I am a manager
- I am an employee
- I am a musician
- I am an artist
- I am an alcoholic
- I am an addict
- I am creative
- I am analytical
- I am adventurous
- I am timid
- I am faithful
- I am confident
- I am funny
- I am anxious
- I am excited
- I am angry
- I am depressed
- I am happy
- I am sad
- I am bad
- I am good

You can think of this sense of 'I am' like a light that illuminates whatever we shine it on. When a person says 'I am Alex', 'I am stuck' or 'I am confident', it's similar to an equal sign, creating an equation in our perception that goes something like this:

$$I = Alex$$
$$I = Stuck$$
$$I = Confident$$

Once we've shone that sense of 'I am' on one of these concepts, it can really feel as though that's who or what we really are. But who you *really* are isn't your name, an emotion or some other label. Who you *really* are is that sense of 'I am'.

> *You are not what you think; you are the thinker.*
> *You are not what the light is shining on; you are the light.*

We're going to be referring to the light of 'I am' as CONSCIOUSNESS: the experience principle.

CONSCIOUSNESS: the experience principle

People are aware. The principle of CONSCIOUSNESS refers to our capacity to have an *experience* of THOUGHT taking form in the moment. CONSCIOUSNESS brings our THOUGHT-generated experiential reality to life.

A few years ago, I was listening to a recording by the philosopher Sydney Banks. Banks was a Scottish welder who had a profound enlightenment experience in 1974, and insightfully realized that there are principles behind human psychology (just as there are principles in the fields of physics or chemistry). Suddenly his words leapt out at me...

> *...if you're searching for happiness; if you're searching for tranquility...*

if you're searching just to have a nice, peaceful,
loving, understanding life...
in actual fact, you're searching for your inner self...

I'd listened to the recording many times before, but this time I really *heard* it.

Whatever you may <u>believe</u> you've been searching
for until now,
what you've <u>really</u> been seeking is your inner self...
What you've been looking <u>for</u>, you've been looking <u>with</u>...
You are the light...

Later that morning, I was riding a rush hour train into central London. The carriage was jam-packed with harassed-looking workers steeling themselves in anticipation of the day ahead. I looked from face to face, imagining what was going on in their minds. Targets to hit, deals to close, conflicts to resolve. People to placate, stresses to manage, obstacles to be avoided or overcome. Results to achieve. Then suddenly it struck me...

We're all searching for our inner selves, but few of us realize it *consciously.*

Your wellbeing

When you were a little child, you likely spent much of your time in a peaceful, contented state of mind. While you probably had many things that temporarily bothered you, you always returned to that place of peace and connection with your inner self; your wellbeing. I'll say that again: Your well *being...* the *well being* that you truly are.

Then somewhere along the way, we were trained to believe that admission to that place of peace and connection was conditional; that it had to be earned, bought or achieved. And that it could be withheld for bad behaviour.

We were conditioned to look outside ourselves for the peace,
happiness and security that can only be found within.

When you're looking to something *outside* yourself for a sense of peace, security or happiness, you're actually trying to find your inner self. And when you're concerned that your peace, security or happiness is at threat from something outside of you, you're believing that it could *stop* you finding your inner self. There's an old put-down that goes something like 'He couldn't hit the water if he fell out of a boat'. It's based on the fact that if you fall overboard, the water is such a big target that it's impossible to miss.

Your inner self is such a big target that it's impossible to miss.

The moment you realize that you already have what you've been searching for until now, you step into a different world. You'll still have results you're inspired to create, and you may use goals, targets or other objectives to achieve them, but where you're 'coming from' – the *feeling* you're living in – is entirely different…

You already are what you've been searching for until now…
What you've been searching for, you've been searching with.

IMPLICATION: You can't be a victim of circumstance

Misunderstanding/Illusion/ Trick of the mind/La-la Land	The reality you're built for/ Fact of life/Pre-existing truth
The outside-in misunderstanding: it can honestly seem as though you are, have been or could be a victim of circumstance. The outside-in illusion can be so compelling that we sometimes feel certain that external circumstances, past occurrences or future events could cause us to feel a certain way	*The inside-out reality:* at the level of principle, it's not possible for you to be a victim of circumstance. Please note: I'm not saying it's not possible for stuff to *happen* to people. I might get a broken leg or a punch in the nose before today is over; it's *definitely* possible for stuff to happen to people. But it's not possible for any of those things to have a particular *emotional impact*. It's not possible for anything in the world of form to have a specific emotional impact. It's not possible for anything in the outside world to damage or harm you psychologically

You are psychologically safe

Here's why there's nothing that can harm you psychologically: You're always living in the feeling of THOUGHT in the moment and always have been, even if you hadn't realized it until now. For the rest of your life, you're never going to feel anything *other than* THOUGHT in the moment. Ever. No matter what. And there's no thinking that can harm you.

This is beautiful because it means you have the ultimate protection built into your psychological and emotional system. It means you're *psychologically* safe from harm or attack.

Reality check

I'm not talking about physical safety – I definitely recommend you wear your seat belt and take appropriate steps to take care of your physical body. But psychologically, it's not possible for you to be harmed. When Mahima was asked what was keeping her safe following the earthquake, she said: 'If you mean physically, I don't know that I *was* safe; we don't know if we are right *now*. Physically, *anything* can happen, right? But I think the thing that was bothering me before I had the insight was not the *physical* lack of safety, because clearly I was alive. It was something *internal*, a felt sense, and it had no relevance to what was happening outside. Because for all you know the roof could fall down; if you don't expect it, you're not afraid because it's not in your thinking in that moment. So that's what my experience of safety was; on the outside nobody knows if you're safe, who knows what's going to happen. But on the inside I didn't need to *feel* unsafe, that was unrelated'.

Don't get me wrong; it's certainly possible for a person to *believe* they're a victim of circumstance. The illusory power of THOUGHT is so convincing and compelling that we all get fooled by it from time to time. The power of THOUGHT gives people the ability to believe all kinds of things, but that doesn't make them true. It's possible for people to believe the earth is flat, but that doesn't mean it actually *is* flat. Similarly, it's possible for us to believe we're victims of circumstance, but you can't actually *be* a victim of circumstance. And as you wake up to the fact of this, you start experiencing greater freedom, clarity and wellbeing.

Practicality check: How is realizing my true nature going to help me get results?

As you fall out of the boat of your contaminated thinking, you can't miss the water of your inner self...

Your inner self is the source of all security,
resilience and courage...
Of all insight, realization and creativity...
Of all passion, purpose and direction...
Of all peace, love and connection...
Of evolution and transformation...
Your inner self is the source of all results.

Your inner self is the source of all results. As you wake up to who you really are, your capacity to create the results that matter to you increases exponentially.

The presence of sanity

Mahima is a scholarship student on my coach training programme, so I took the opportunity to interview her about her extraordinary experience. As I chatted with Mahima in front of the group, one of the other participants asked if she'd been teaching these principles to other survivors of the earthquake. Mahima replied that she hadn't been teaching them *explicitly*, but that the presence of sane human beings has a positive effect in its own right; that her realization that she was psychologically safe meant she was free to serve others in whatever ways made sense. She later wrote, 'In the eight months since the earthquake in Nepal, I have seen the broad and all-pervasive relevance of these principles. An understanding of the foundational principles behind how we function as human beings and "how life works" changes everything from career planning and good governance to crisis response and parenting. It takes us beyond trauma and problem-solving to experiencing the full spectrum of a rich human life'.

The presence of sane human beings has a positive effect in its own right.

You are already mentally healthy; psychologically whole and resilient. The source of emotional intelligence is already right there within you. The only thing that *ever* gets in the way is the mistaken belief that we're feeling something *other than* THOUGHT in the moment. We each have mental health and wellbeing at our core, with the wisdom and common sense to make good decisions. So how do you decide which results are worth investing your time, energy and resources in? In a nutshell: How do you know what to want?

> **Bottom line results:** For many people, work occupies a large amount of their time, energy and focus. As you become more deeply acquainted with 'who you really are', you start freeing yourself from the delusion that your happiness, security and wellbeing are dependent on (or can be threatened by) your job, your results or your ambitions. Paradoxically, as you *subtract* that delusion, your increasing clarity releases huge amounts of energy for you to enjoy your current circumstances, while focusing your energies on creating the results that matter to you.
>
>
>
> **CLARITY**   plus   **ACTION**   equals   **RESULTS**
>
> Figure 4.1:   The CLARITY® Results Model

keep exploring ⁜ connect with others
share your discoveries ⁜ deepen your understanding

Experiment: Say 'I am <your name>', either aloud or to yourself. Notice whatever sense of 'I am-ness' you become aware of. You have a name, but you are not your name; you're the one who is experiencing this name. You have a body, but you are not your body; you're the one who is experiencing this body. You have many thoughts, but you are not your thoughts; you're the one who is experiencing these thoughts. I encourage you to reflect on the notion that who you <u>really</u> are is that formless, indestructible and ever-present purity of 'I am'... the principle of CONSCIOUSNESS.

www.jamiesmart.com/results4

5

Finding Your Place of Meaning, Passion and Purpose

If you don't know where you're going...
Any road will take you there...

George Harrison
Musician, film producer

'What's your purpose in life?'

I was attending a workshop in 2007, and the trainer had invited us to direct this question to the person sitting next to us. When I was asked, I trotted out something I'd come up with a few months earlier, but it no longer rang true. I told my partner, 'That doesn't feel right; I have to be true to myself'. I tried several times to get my 'pre-prepared purpose' to fit, but each time it sounded hollow and empty. Finally, I approached the trainer and told him there was something wrong; that each time I spoke my purpose, it felt 'off'. 'I have to be true to myself', I repeated for the fifth time, before suddenly realizing what I'd said. In that moment, wisdom was speaking…

You have to be true to yourself.
This is your purpose right now; to be true to yourself.
To be guided by intuition, realization and authentic desire.

This is the essence of the shift from a life driven by the conditioning of the past to one guided through connection with your own authenticity; to the living wisdom of the moment. Wisdom is constantly guiding us, if only we have the ears to hear its gentle urging.

While I'd been looking *outside* myself, trying to figure out some suitably grand purpose, the voice of the *inner* self was speaking the simple fact of my purpose in that moment… *You have to be true to yourself*. You see, it turns out that you don't find your *purpose*; purpose finds *you*. In this chapter, you're going to be getting in touch with your inner source of evolutionary purpose; the guidance system that can keep you on track today, and 20 years from today.

Exponential organizations and the power of purpose

While researching his groundbreaking book, *Exponential Organizations*, angel investor Salim Ismail and his team explored businesses that were growing at an exponential rate (e.g. Airbnb, Netflix, Uber each doubled the size of their business in 2015). One of the qualities they identified that all the exponential organizations share is a 'massive transformational purpose' (MTP). You may be familiar with some of these, for instance...

- TED's MTP is to spread ideas.

- Uber's MTP is to evolve the way the world moves.

- Kickstarter's MTP is to help bring creative projects to life.

- Duolingo's MTP is to give everyone access to education of the highest quality – for free.

- LinkedIn's MTP is to create economic opportunity for every member of the global workforce.

- Google's MTP is to organize the world's information and make it universally accessible and useful.

Millennials are flocking to purpose-driven companies. A recent survey* of LinkedIn employees showed that over 40% of them prioritized meaning and fulfilment *above* wages and job status. Research shows that purpose-oriented employees are far more likely to be high performers, with strong levels of engagement and loyalty to the purpose-driven organizations that employ them.

*Reported in the blog post *The Power of Purpose at Work* by Reid Hoffman, Nov 6th 2015

Your inner source of evolutionary purpose

While you may not be founding an exponential-growth business, a sense of purpose and direction are innate; as natural to you as breathing. When you were a child, a purpose would find you, captivate you and guide you until you transcended it. This is the sense of evolutionary purpose that has already motivated you...

- To crawl, to walk and to talk.

- To explore the world and learn about what fascinates you.

- To throw yourself into pastimes, hobbies and other activities.

- To develop skills and master them.

A purpose finds you, captivates you, then guides you until you transcend it.

That sense of evolutionary purpose is what has me writing this book, and may well be what has you reading it. Stop and consider that for a moment. Are you open to the possibility that your innate capacity for purpose and direction is guiding you *in this very moment*?

As you reflect on your life, you may be able to identify a number of different times or periods when you were captured by a particular passion, purpose or enthusiasm. In fact, the word 'enthusiasm' comes from ancient Greek, and literally translates as 'the God within'. The ancients recognized the wisdom of your passions, enthusiasms and authentic desires.

So what gets in the way of realizing your purpose?

There's an old Sufi tale about the wise man, Nasruddin, who was observed one day racing his donkey through the streets of Baghdad, frantically searching for something. The townsfolk called out, asking what he'd lost. Nasruddin shouted, 'I'm looking for my donkey!'

You may have been told you need to 'find your purpose', but how do you do that? It turns out that a more valuable question to ask is, 'What gets in the way of your *realizing* purpose?' What gets in the way is looking for it where it isn't...

The misguided search for purpose is the biggest obstacle to finding it.

It turns out there's only one thing that ever gets in the way of you knowing what's right for you in the moment: contaminated thinking. The source of contaminated thinking is the outside-in misunderstanding; the mistaken belief that you're feeling something *other than* THOUGHT in the moment.

Your feelings don't know anything about your character,
your circumstances or your sense of direction.
Your feelings only ever know about THOUGHT
in the moment.

You can't find something where it isn't

Consider these phrases:

- 'I'm stuck. I've lost my sense of purpose'.

- 'I'm looking for my purpose'.

- 'I'm trying to find a sense of direction in my life'.

They imply that 'purpose' is something external; something you can find, have, lose or lack. If purpose was a material object (like a pen, a phone or a bunch of keys), then losing it and looking for it would make sense. But your purpose is not a material object. It's a fresh new thought that arrives as an insight; a realization that brings you closer to the reality of life that you're part of.

Imagine a whirlpool or eddy in a fast-flowing river. While you could name the whirlpool and describe its characteristics, it has no existence independent of the river. While you can *perceive* the whirlpool as distinct and separate for practical purposes, it is never *actually* separate. The whirlpool is inseparable from the river, part of an undivided whole.

While you have a name and can describe your characteristics,
you have no existence independent of the oneness of life.
While you can perceive yourself as distinct and separate for
practical purposes, you are never <u>actually</u> separate.
You are inseparable from the intelligence and oneness of life,
part of an undivided whole.

We'll be referring to the oneness of life as the principle of MIND. You, your life and your purpose in the moment are all an expression of this formless principle.

MIND: the power principle

People are alive. The principle of MIND is the 'intelligent energy' that shows up in all aspects of the natural world. MIND is the 'power source' behind life. Various cultures and fields have different names for this power: Life force, universal energy, chi, nature, the great spirit, God, the no-thing, evolution, random chance etc. You can think of it in whatever way makes sense to you.

So what is 'purpose'?

Purpose is a thought, and like all thoughts, it comes with a feeling. Your evolutionary purpose is less likely to be something you 'figure out' so much as something you glimpse or *realize*; a function of your innate capacity for insight. When you have such a realization, it may have some of these qualities…

- It may come with a feeling of gentle certainty or knowing.

- It may come as a sudden flash of realization, or as a slow awakening.

- It may strike you as extremely obvious, with an 'Of course! How did I not see this before?' quality.

So how do you create the conditions for this kind of realization?

Stop looking for it where it isn't.

Of course, this doesn't just apply to purpose; it applies to *all* our innate qualities. When we look outside ourselves for that which can only be found within us, it sets up an 'outside-in' dynamic that generates contaminated thinking. But when we *subtract* that misunderstanding, our innate capacities emerge. Do you remember the *CLARITY® Equation* from Chapter 2? Here's a slightly expanded version of it.

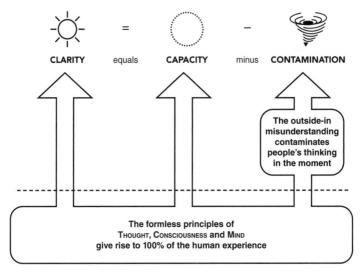

| CLARITY | equals | CAPACITY | minus | CONTAMINATION |

The outside-in misunderstanding contaminates people's thinking in the moment

The formless principles of
THOUGHT, CONSCIOUSNESS and MIND
give rise to 100% of the human experience

Figure 5.1:   The Principles Behind the CLARITY® Equation

We're always living in the feeling of the principle of THOUGHT taking form, moment to moment. THOUGHT creates your perceptual reality and CONSCIOUSNESS gives you an experience of the totality of your THOUGHT-generated perceptual reality in the moment. Your whole experience, moment to moment, is powered by the principle of MIND.

A paradigm for psychology

MIND, THOUGHT and CONSCIOUSNESS are the principles behind human psychological functioning, first articulated by Sydney Banks. While they're pointing in the same direction as many wisdom traditions of the past, Banks was able to go further, stating them as 'principles' in the scientific sense of the word (i.e. fundamental laws of reality such as the principle of gravity). Whenever humanity discovers the foundational principles behind a field, it creates a shared basis of agreement for future explorations which then *transforms* that field. The shared basis for agreement is referred to as the field's 'paradigm'.

- Newton's *realization* of the principle of gravity formed the basis for a paradigm that transformed the field of physics.

- Lavoisier's *realization* of the principles behind combustion formed the basis for a paradigm that transformed the field of chemistry.

- Semmelweis' *realization* of germ theory formed the basis for a paradigm that transformed the field of medicine.

Sydney Banks insightfully realized and articulated the foundational principles behind psychology; principles that form the basis of a paradigm for a field that has been awash with conflicting ideas, concepts and theories until now.

- Banks' realization of the principles behind human psychological functioning form the basis for a paradigm that will transform the field of psychology.

Your perception is like a desktop

In his fascinating TED talk, *Do We See Reality As It Is?* cognitive neuroscientist Donald Hoffman uses your computer's desktop as a metaphor for perception. He explains that we don't see reality 'as it is'. Rather, what we experience is an internally generated model, informed in part by our sensory data. We can think of time and space as our desktop, and the various 'objects' in our world (e.g. bananas, buildings, bodies) as symbols or *icons* on that desktop. Just as there are implications to interacting with an icon on your computer or smartphone, there are implications to interacting with the 'icons' in your world (e.g. people, pythons, poppadoms). 100% of your computer's desktop and the icons are generated from within the deeper properties of the device. Similarly, 100% of the desktop and icons of your perception (i.e. space, time and the physical and non-physical forms/objects you perceive) are generated from within the deeper properties of life. These deeper properties are by definition formless, i.e. they are what *generates* the forms of your perception (the desktop and icons). At the end of his talk, Hoffman says...

> *When I have a perceptual experience that I describe as a brain, or neurons, I am interacting with reality, but that reality is not a brain or neurons and is nothing like a brain or neurons.*

And that reality, whatever it is, is the real source of cause and effect in the world – not brains, not neurons. Brains and neurons have no causal powers. They cause none of our perceptual experiences, and none of our behavior.

The metaphors of MIND, THOUGHT and CONSCIOUSNESS are a way of referring to the deeper reality Hoffman is pointing to... the real source of cause and effect in the world and in your life. The principles of MIND, THOUGHT and CONSCIOUSNESS generate your perceptual reality *and* the sense of a 'you' that is experiencing it.

Purpose can give you a glimpse of the future

In late 2008, I was feeling off-track. My most recent purpose had found me and guided me, but I'd transcended it and I was feeling frustrated and directionless. Then, I started exploring the principles behind clarity. As my understanding deepened, my head started to clear and I had a series of realizations. The first realization came to me while I was asleep and dreaming...

Everything you've been looking for outside *of you is actually to be found* within *you.*
External results can be wonderful, but they can't give you a feeling.

I awoke with a start, feeling better than I could remember feeling in months. I'd suddenly realized that peace, security and fulfilment can never be found in external circumstances and accomplishments. While external results can be *wonderful*, they can't give you a feeling; that can only come from *within* you. The second realization arrived a few weeks later...

The fact that you can perceive <u>anything</u> means you have the source of peace, fulfilment and wellbeing

> *already within you. You already have the ingredients*
> *of a high-quality experiential lifestyle.*

This shocked me, and had an immediate impact on my work with clients. When you know with absolute certainty that a person is fundamentally OK, it influences how you experience that person and how they experience you. *The presence of sane human beings has a positive effect in its own right...*

Practicality check: How is understanding purpose going to help me get results?

A deeper understanding of the nature of purpose can have a powerful impact in a number of ways...

- It clears your mind of the contaminated thinking that fills people's heads when they're looking for their purpose.

- This creates a space for wisdom, realization and trusting your authentic desires.

- As purpose finds you, it becomes easier to make decisions about how to invest your time, energy and other resources.

- When you authentically share your purpose with others, it's like you become a tuning fork. People who resonate with you are drawn to you and your message.

- Purpose is one of the most powerful qualifiers there is for helping people choose whether they want to be 'on your team', and helping you decide whether or not they're a good fit.

- The *feeling* of purpose and direction is a powerful energy in its own right, and can awaken courage, motivation and resolve.

The third insight arrived a month after that, and revealed something truly extraordinary. You see, purpose can give you a glimpse of a possible future.

Bottom line results: Every successful organization is founded with a sense of purpose and direction, but many lose touch with it over time. Or the world changes, but the organization's purpose doesn't evolve. A felt sense of purpose can inspire passion, loyalty and motivation in the people who resonate with it. In fact, purpose-oriented employees are far more likely to be high performers, with strong levels of engagement. As you become more attuned to the subtle signals of purpose, you'll find yourself tapping into its power for yourself and others, more and more easily.

keep exploring ⁘ connect with others
share your discoveries ⁘ deepen your understanding

Experiment: Open to the possibility that you've already been guided by a sense of purpose and direction your whole life. You started with learning to crawl, walk and talk. At some points you may have been very aware of the guiding hand of purpose; at other points less so. Are you open to the possibility that your decision to read this book is guided by a deeper sense of purpose and direction in your life? After all, you chose it for a reason. What would happen if you were to experiment with letting go of the search for purpose, and relaxing into the knowledge that it's already guiding you perfectly?

www.jamiesmart.com/results5

6

Leadership: The Inner Key to Confidence and Certainty

*You don't need to put the yolk in the egg.
The yolk is already in the egg.*

Valda Monroe
Educator, single-paradigm pioneer

'These principles are to psychology what the discovery of germs was to medicine...'

The realization hit me the moment I woke up. It was the spring of 2009, and I'd been exploring the principles behind clarity for six months. I'd seen some big changes in my own life and in the lives of my clients. But until that morning, I'd been relating to these principles as an approach, intervention or methodology; as yet another tool for my (already crowded) toolbox. The realization that these were actually principles – fundamental laws of reality – changed everything, and it took my breath away...

The principles behind clarity represent the future of psychology...
These principles are to psychology what the discovery of germs was to medicine.

The moment I saw this, I knew I was going to be exploring and sharing these principles for the next 20 years. Just as the acceptance of germ theory had a massive impact on the *physical* health of humanity, the widespread realization of these principles would have a massive impact on the *psychological* health of humanity. I felt inspired, with a sense of clarity and motivation. Purpose had found me and given me a glimpse of the future. My priorities changed in a heartbeat; it was clear what I had to do... 'You have to get a deeper understanding of these principles, and start sharing them with people'.

And that's when I started feeling insecure. An explosion of thoughts crowded into my mind...

- Who did I think I was, claiming to know the future of psychology? I'd dropped out of university and didn't even have a *degree*.

- Why just 20 years? If I was serious about it, surely I would be committed to doing this for the rest of my life.

- Who was I to be telling people they had the source of security, wisdom and wellbeing already within them? I was a habitual worrier, with a variety of personal issues.

Fortunately, I'd caught 'the leadership bug' many years earlier, so I was no stranger to the feelings of insecurity that often follow on the heels of inspiration (sometimes referred to as 'impostor syndrome'). By the time you've finished this chapter, you'll have caught the leadership bug too, as you get more in touch with your *inner* source of leadership; the key to courage, confidence and certainty.

You are already a leader

Whether you're the CEO of a Fortune 500 company… or you're currently on welfare… or (like most people reading this book) you're somewhere else along that spectrum…

You have the innate capacities of leadership within you…
You are already a leader…

You are already connected to your *inner* source of leadership, and (whether you're aware of it or not) you've already had times in your life when you've demonstrated this fact.

The Emergency Alert System

It was less than 48 hours since the attempted assassination of President Ronald Reagan, and there was still a palpable sense of alarm and unease in the aftermath of the shooting. My parents were sitting in the front seats of our rental car as we waited at a traffic light outside the historic town of Lahaina (I was 15 years old, and my family were visiting Hawaii for spring break). Suddenly my parents went rigid with fear as the shriek of an air raid siren filled our senses. The purpose of the *Emergency Alert System* (EAS) is to warn islanders of approaching tsunamis and other potential emergencies. 'Turn on the radio', I said, but my parents remained frozen. The second time, I raised my voice and barked a command, 'Turn on the radio!' My father snapped out of his paralysis and turned the dial, where we discovered that the sirens were part of the monthly *test* of the EAS. There was no emergency.

My parents both grew up in the UK during World War II, and the sound of an air raid siren meant one thing: bombs. When they heard the Maui sirens, their heads filled up with contaminated thinking. They were in La-la Land, immobilized with panic. But I didn't have that thinking; my head was clear. I was present in the moment, hanging out in the reality we're all built for. Tuning in to the radio was common sense. It would have been just as obvious to my parents if they hadn't been lost in contaminated thinking arising from the outside-in misunderstanding; the mistaken belief that their feelings were alerting them to something *other than* THOUGHT in the moment. I was tapped into the natural source of leadership we are *all* connected to.

When you've got nothing on your mind, you're a natural leader.
When you're hanging out in reality, leadership is common sense.

When are you a leader?

'What are some of the times and situations in your life when you've shown up as a leader?' I've asked this question to countless participants on my workshops and programmes. At first, people sometimes protest that they don't *have* any examples. But as they relax and listen to other people recount their experiences, their own leadership stories emerge...

- The teenage boy who saved his brother from choking while their mother watched helplessly.

- The intern whose stroke of insight saved their company tens of thousands of pounds.

- The young girl who stepped in when another child was being picked on and stared the bullies down.

They often say 'I didn't think of that as being a leader; it just seemed *obvious*'. These examples may seem like anomalies – too rare or too small to 'qualify' as leadership – but they reveal its essence...

*When we're caught up in contaminated thinking, we look to
others, trying to figure out what to do.
When you've got nothing on your mind, your innate
leadership qualities emerge effortlessly.*

DISTINCTION: Additive approaches vs subtractive understanding

In his fascinating book, *Antifragile*, bestselling author and risk analyst Nassim Nicholas Taleb explains that we tend to be suckers for 'positive advice'; the **additive approaches** offered by how-to books, government interventions, crash diets, medication prescriptions, get-rich-quick schemes etc. For a simple example of additive approaches, look at the 'top tips' articles featured on the covers of many popular magazines...

- The 5 keys to six-pack abs
- The 7 tips for finding Mr Right
- 21 mind-blowing sex moves

- 8 ways to build muscle fast
- 6 steps to sexy hair
- 7 career moves to make you unbeatable

- The 5 keys to financial freedom
- 7 steps to a swimsuit body
- The 6 secrets of successful relationships

- 17 essential looks for summer
- The 5 rules of creating wealth

When people are looking for additive approaches, they're asking the question, 'What do I need to add to my life/myself/my skills/my personality to make me more X and less Y?' The structure of the additive approach is always the same:

You + Additive Approach = Super You

This seductive and compelling promise is like crack cocaine to our insecurities. It's the driver behind the hundreds of millions of dollars made from 'success', 'get rich quick' and 'how to x,y,z fast' materials each year. This promise is the reason behind the colossal appetite for self-help books. It's why those magazines can put seven new tips on each month's cover.

When we're feeling insecure, we're compelled by the notion of an additive approach. But there's a problem...

Additive approaches rarely work

In practice additive approaches rarely deliver the hoped-for results, and can even cause actual harm. For instance, in the USA, it's estimated that iatrogenic illness (illness caused accidentally by medical interventions) is *the third biggest killer* after heart disease and cancer. The 2012 arrest of 200 UK gang leaders under the banner of the government's 'all-out war on gangs and gang culture' backfired and created a dangerous power vacuum, with even more ruthless youngsters jockeying for position. When you read the seven top tips (or whatever), they instantly strike you as obvious ('Why didn't I think of that? I really should do that') and are often forgotten the next instant. Why?

> *Additive advice without embodied understanding*
> *has little or no effect.*

For example, doctors and nurses in the 1800s had to be *forced* to wash their hands, because they didn't have an understanding of germ theory. Once you understand the reality of germs, washing your hands is just common sense. *Until* you understand the reality of germs, it's just one more chore on an already long list.

Subtraction is the secret of leadership

The secret to leading yourself and others is subtraction. As I mentioned in Chapter 3, the CLARITY® model is ruthlessly **subtractive**.

| CLARITY | equals | CAPACITY | minus | CONTAMINATION |

Figure 6.1: The CLARITY® Equation

Clarity is your natural state of mind when there's no contaminated thinking getting in the way. When you've got nothing on your mind, your innate leadership qualities emerge effortlessly. When people first see this, they typically look for another additive approach, and ask 'OK, how do I stop thinking so much? How do I get rid of my contaminated thinking?' Surprisingly, the answer to this question isn't addition, but *subtraction*. A more leveraged question turns out to be 'What's been giving rise to the contaminated thinking in the first place?' After all, if we can identify the 'cause' of that thinking, we can address *that* and cut it off at the source! So what's the cause?

Misunderstanding contaminates

To answer that question, let's use physical health as an analogy. The human body has an incredible capacity for healing wounds, as long as the wound is free from contamination by germs and bacteria. In the 1830s, surgeons innocently infected their patients by operating on them with dirty scalpels in filthy operating theatres (nineteenth-century operating theatres were typically so dirty that the smell was almost unbearable). Surgeons had a misunderstanding about the cause of infection, and that misunderstanding gave rise to countless unintentional contaminations. Similarly, our misunderstanding of the cause of our experience ('the outside-in misunderstanding') gives rise to the 'contaminant' of misinformed thinking.

Understanding is subtractive

Subtracting a misunderstanding, and getting more closely aligned with reality, has a profound effect. Ignaz Semmelweis' insights about the nature of germs and bacteria have resulted in a 30-year increase in the average lifespan of every person on the planet. Seeing through this misunderstanding about how life *already works* has had a bigger effect on physical wellbeing than *all medical interventions combined*.

The harmful effects of the outside-in misunderstanding are infinitely more devastating than the combined benefits of every tip, technique, methodology, intervention or psychiatric medication ever developed. Seeing through the outside-in misunderstanding can provide enormous psychological benefit. And as your psychology is behind all your decisions, performances and results, the impact on your life as a whole can be truly profound.

> *Getting a deeper understanding of the principles behind clarity unlocks your innate leadership qualities. . .*
> *The source of confidence, certainty and results.*

Leadership is something you catch In my first book, *CLARITY*, I explained the difference between symptoms and causes as follows:

DISTINCTION: Symptoms vs causes

Acting like you have the symptoms of a cold is difficult and unconvincing. But when you *have* a cold, the bug causes the symptoms to emerge effortlessly and authentically. Most leadership books and programmes make a valiant effort to help people master the symptoms of leadership; behaviours, skills and attitudes, modelled from successful leaders (some of them extremely successful). Unfortunately, acting like you have the *symptoms* of leadership is difficult and unconvincing, because the symptoms aren't what's doing the 'heavy lifting'. But when you have the 'leadership bug', it causes the symptoms to emerge effortlessly and authentically. The real power source is the cause that gives *rise* to the symptoms.

The deep drivers are your innate leadership qualities

So what's the cause that gives rise to the symptoms of leadership? The formless principles of MIND, CONSCIOUSNESS and THOUGHT. These principles create 100% of your moment-to-moment experience. When contaminated thinking is subtracted, they show up as your entrepreneurial superpowers; the eight deep drivers we mentioned in Chapter 1. These innate qualities are the source of emotional intelligence and authentic leadership...

Direction: A sense of direction, purpose and motivation, free from urgency and undue pressure. Setting out to create a result requires a sense of direction, especially if you want to involve other people in that result.

Resilience: A strong sense of inner resilience, security and trust in yourself in life. Resilience is essential for dealing with the ups and downs of life, allowing you to navigate change and thrive through uncertainty. It's the deep driver behind why some people and organizations bounce back in the face of setbacks, while others struggle to recover.

Creativity: A reliable source of creativity, insight and inspired ideas. Creativity is the driver behind all problem-solving and an essential power source when it comes to creating results.

Authenticity: The freedom to be yourself, speak your truth and do what you know to be right. As well as being fundamental to discerning your authentic desires, 'knowing yourself' and walking your talk is also one of the keys to drawing other people to your cause if you want to involve others in the results you're creating.

Intuition: Alignment with your intuition and inner wisdom, your internal guidance system. Whether you call it intuition, wisdom or 'gut feel', extraordinary results-creators from Thomas Edison and Richard Branson to Oprah Winfrey and Steve Jobs have acknowledged it as one of the key drivers in creating results.

Presence: Present, aware and available to the moment, connected with your mind, your body and the world around you. Presence is a rare quality, but when someone has it, other people sit up and take notice. As well as being a key to influence, presence brings with it playful curiosity, charisma and enhanced awareness, making it particularly useful when it comes to creating results.

Connection: Warm, genuine connections with other people, leading to stronger relationships with clients, colleagues, friends, family members and lovers. Strong relationships are important, particularly when your results involve other people.

Clarity: A clear mind, free from contaminated thinking, fully present and in the moment, with the levels of performance, satisfaction and enjoyment that brings. We live in a world of increasing volatility, uncertainty, complexity and ambiguity. Clarity is the ability to discern the factors that make a difference and act on them productively, without being distracted by the 'noise' in the system.

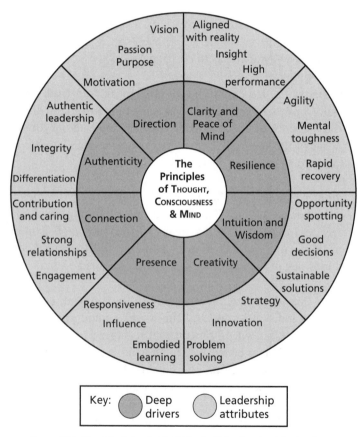

Figure 6.2: The Principles Behind Clarity Drive Leadership Attributes

Practicality check: How is being a leader going to help me get results?

Being a results-creator *means* being a leader...

- It means venturing into the unknown, and making your own path.

- It means facing your insecurities and risking failure.

- It means braving the fear of criticism.

- It means developing your creative muscles, experimenting and taking risks.

- It means realizing that you're *already* a leader and understanding where the source of leadership exists.

We started this chapter talking about the realization that the principles behind clarity represent the future of psychology. That one realization captivated me and has been guiding me ever since. It had me sell the business I'd spent so much time and energy developing, turn my back on the field I'd become a leader in and move in an entirely new direction. The fact that the book you're reading even *exists* is a result of that realization. So when you have a realization, how do you know what to do next?

Bottom line results: Leadership is a business essential. The qualities of leadership are innate, but good leaders *appear* to be in short supply. Why? While everyone has innate leadership capacities, they're often obscured by contaminated thinking (e.g. fear of failure, of criticism, of the unknown, of responsibility, of public speaking) But as you realize this for yourself, you'll find contaminated thinking being subtracted and your innate leadership capacities emerging. You'll also discover that these facts make it easier to realize the leadership potential in others.

keep exploring ⁘ connect with others
share your discoveries ⁘ deepen your understanding

Experiment: Who do you think of as a great leader? Someone who inspires you? Someone you admire? Are you open to the possibility that you already have the same leadership capacities as they do? That you are already connected to the same source of authentic leadership? As you reflect on this possibility, you might like to consider this question... What are some of the times and situations in your life when you are (or have been) a leader?

www.jamiesmart.com/results6

7

The Liberating Truth About Goals

Integrity has no need of rules.

Albert Camus
Journalist, author, winner of the Nobel Prize in Literature, 1957

'A study of the 1953 graduates of Yale University clearly demonstrates this point…'

In his bestselling book, *Unlimited Power*, Anthony Robbins describes a study of the Yale University Class of 1953 and the follow-up, 20 years later. He explains that the 3% of the class who had clear written goals and a plan for achieving them were more financially successful by 1973 than the other 97% of the class combined. In addition, he reports that the 3% scored more highly on measures such as happiness and joy. Robbins uses this study as proof of the power of goal setting, stating that 'the difference in people's abilities to fully tap their personal resources is directly affected by their goals'.

When I read Robbins' book in 1999, I saw where I'd been going wrong. I hadn't set the kind of bold, audacious goals I clearly needed if I wanted to live a truly outstanding life. I started following the instructions in the book, asking myself what I really wanted. I made my goals clear and specific, and created a detailed vision of my future. I envisaged a life of passion and purpose, with health, happiness and financial freedom. The vision included me and my family, the kind of house we'd be living in and the business that would support us. Five years later, I'd left my job and had built a successful business. We were living with our two young daughters in a large house very much like the one I'd envisioned. The plan appeared to be working.

That's when my wife told me she wanted a divorce, and my world fell apart…

I'll be happy when… Wholesome… Secure… Successful… Passionate… Peaceful… Fulfilled… Free…

I had believed that if I could create a life like the one I'd *envisaged*, then I'd finally feel the way I wanted to *feel*. I'd been running on the 'I'll be happy when…' hamster wheel without even realizing it, in thrall to the outside-in misunderstanding. I was so preoccupied with future results that I was oblivious to the beauty of the present moment. There's only one problem with the oft-mentioned *Yale University Goals Study*...

It never actually happened...

Despite investigative efforts by *Fast Company* magazine and an in-depth search of Yale alumni archives, no trace could be found of it. Yale University has since stated *categorically* that no such study of the class of 1953 ever occurred. The likely explanation appears to be that the 1953 Yale study was such a compelling *story* that many of the world's best-known motivational speakers of the day used it to validate 'success systems' based on audacious goals, unwavering self-belief and massive action.

I'm not blaming Robbins and his ilk for my mistakes; my choices and decisions were my own. But it turns out that much of the 'received wisdom' about goal setting is nonsense, grounded in the outside-in misunderstanding. By the time you've finished this chapter, you'll see goals for what they are, and understand how you can use them in the context of a far more powerful and sophisticated 'success system' you've been benefiting from your whole life.

A goal is a thought

When people talk about goals, they're usually thinking in terms of a specific result they want to achieve. But what is a goal? *A goal is a thought; nothing more.* Any feeling you get when you think about a goal is telling you about your THOUGHT-generated perceptual reality in that moment, *not* about the *result* you're imagining. While a goal can be a useful tool (e.g. for helping you set a direction, organize your efforts or coordinate the efforts of a group of people), it has no power in and of itself.

You have an innate capacity for achieving goals

You set and achieve goals every day. Tasks as mundane as brushing your teeth, going for a walk or making a hot drink involve complex nested structures of goals, actions and evidence criteria. We employ these structures automatically without even thinking about it consciously. When viewed through the lens of 'goal achievement', making a cup of tea involves having a goal for some purpose, taking some action and meeting some evidence of completion.

Goal	*What do you want? (A cup of tea)*
Purpose	*Why do you want that? (I'm thirsty and want a hot drink)*
Evidence criteria	*How will you know you've got it? (My thirst will be quenched and I will feel satisfied)*
Action	*What needs to happen for that to happen? (Make and drink tea)*

But if you look at it more closely, the action 'Make and drink tea' is itself composed of a number of goals, each with their own evidence and action (e.g. boil water, put teabag in cup, pour water on teabag, allow tea to brew, add milk, drink tea). If we looked even more closely, each of these would be composed of yet more goals with *their* own evidence and action.

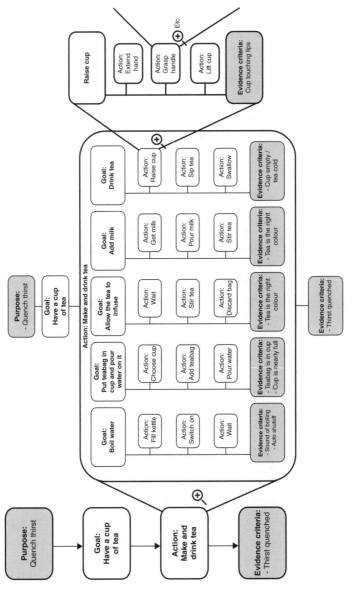

Figure 7.1: Embodied Understanding Drives Results-creation

Reality check

'Great!' I hear you say, 'I'm delighted that I have an amazing system that can help me make a cup of tea whenever I want one. But how is knowing this going to help me create the results I want, and enjoy the process?' Here's how. The capacity that allows you to make a cup of tea without thinking about it is the same capacity that is going to support you in creating the results that matter to you: *embodied understanding*. When we have embodied understanding of a domain, we engage the complex network of relationships that allows us to get *results* in that context.

You're said to have embodied understanding of a domain when you understand it at such a deep level, you don't even have to think about it. For instance, your embodied understanding of gravity helps you to walk, run, jump and negotiate crowded streets effortlessly. Your ability to create results in a given domain is a function of your embodied understanding of the *reality* of that domain. A person who has a deep embodied understanding of tennis is far more likely to win a match than someone who's never held a racquet. A person who has a deep embodied understanding of driving is likely to be a better driver than someone who's never been behind the wheel. Trailblazing artists like Dali, Picasso and Van Gogh produced work that was shocking and often outrageous in its time, but it was grounded in technical mastery and a deep understanding of their art form. So what does this have to do with the results you want to create? Here's what:

Your ability to create results that are a perfect fit for you and your life is a function of your embodied understanding of how your mind works.

Just as an athlete's embodied understanding of gravity will determine the quality of their athletic results, and a doctor's embodied understanding of anatomy will have an influence on the quality of their interventions...

Your understanding of how your mind and perception work have an across-the-board influence on your ability to create the results that matter to you.

You see, the purpose of this book isn't *just* to help you create results; the purpose is also to help you enjoy your life, deepen your connections with others and experience an increasing sense of resilience and wellbeing, every step of the way.

You are already a results-creator

There are already numerous places in your life where you're able to create the results you want, often without even thinking about it. These are some of the areas where you're *already* well aligned with reality. And then there are other areas where it may have been a struggle until now. Those are the areas where you're likely *not* so well aligned with reality. It's easy to think of examples...

- The mother who manages to juggle a hectic family schedule, but can't seem to achieve a healthy bodyweight.

- The entrepreneur who makes money easily, but who struggles with their intimate relationships.

- The therapist who has a profound impact on their clients, but lives hand-to-mouth with no stable income.

- The company director who inspires loyalty and hard work in their people, but struggles with addictive behaviours.

- The analyst who's really good at their job, but yearns to do something else and doesn't know what.

Toxic goals

Toxic goals are goals grounded in the outside-in misunderstanding. They typically have an 'I'll be happy when...' or 'I can't be happy until...' structure, for instance...

- I'll be happy and fulfilled when I have a baby.

- I'll feel successful once I earn a million dollars.

- I can't be happy until I leave this boring job and find work I love.

- I'll feel secure once I'm married.

- I'll be confident once I've lost the weight.

- I can't feel free until I have a location-independent lifestyle.

- I'll feel successful once our share price hits $100.

These are all based around the false belief that our feelings are giving us information about our (future) circumstances. 'Hedonic forecasting' is the name given to our ability to predict how we're going to feel in future circumstances. It turns out that people are very poor judges of their future emotional state. Why? Because we get tricked by the outside-in misunderstanding. We innocently attribute our feelings to something *other than* THOUGHT in the moment. The second we do that, we're at risk of setting a toxic goal. Consider this imaginary conversation…

Karen: I feel stressed.	(The feeling of stress is a signal that Karen's in stressful thinking. This is a healthy and useful signal.)
Bob: Why?	(Bob innocently invites her to blame something other than THOUGHT in the moment; to step into La-la Land.)
Karen: I've got too much to do and not enough time to do it in.	(Karen innocently and mistakenly assigns her feelings to an external factor. She is now in La-la Land.)
Bob: That sucks. What are you going to do about it?	(Bob validates her mistake.)
Karen: Find a job that's not so stressful.	(Because Karen believes her feelings are coming from an external factor, it makes sense to look to the outside if she wants to change how she feels. This is a recipe for a toxic goal.)

So am I saying Karen shouldn't find a new job? No. I have no idea whether she should find a new job or not. But here's what I *do* know:

> *When you're looking at the world from a place of*
> *misunderstanding, the goals you come up with will*
> *reflect that misunderstanding.*
> *When you're looking at the world from a place of clarity, the*
> *goals you come up with will reflect that clarity.*

The transformation of my terrible life

In January 2014, I returned home after a winter holiday, excited to implement some of the fresh new ideas I'd had while I was away. But on my first day back at work, I felt miserable and stuck. The energy and optimism of just 24 hours earlier had been replaced with a pessimistic malaise. I felt awful. So, in an attempt to figure out why I was feeling so bad, I started to look at my life: I thought about my work... and my relationships... and my financial situation... and my health... and what I'm like as a person. And the more I thought, the worse my situation looked. I started to worry. Why had I felt so inspired and motivated? Couldn't I see what a mess my life was in? The situation was dire. It was time to make some big changes and get my life on track. I needed a plan... to set some goals... I needed a system or formula I could use to dig myself out of this mess. I was about to jump on Amazon.com to see if I could find the book that would help me transform my terrible life, when a question floated gently across my consciousness...

Where do you believe your feelings are coming from?

The question stopped me in my tracks, and my head went quiet. The questioning continued... Were you believing your feelings were coming from your health... your relationships... your finances? Were you believing your feelings were letting you know about your future... your past... what you're like as a person? That's *exactly* what I'd been believing. I'd been hanging out in La-la Land, an imaginary world we all visit from time to time... a world where we believe our feelings can tell us about something *other than* THOUGHT in the present moment. But it doesn't work that way; it never has and it never will. I'd woken up in a bad mood (a THOUGHT-generated perceptual reality), that's all. Remember. . .

Your feelings are giving you feedback about the 'glasses' you're currently wearing, not what you're looking at.

The moment I realized this, my 'terrible life' was transformed. I still didn't feel great, but I was no longer confused about where my feelings were coming from. I'd fallen out of La-la Land and back into reality. I decided to start working through my 'to-do' list. A little while later, it occurred to me to take a break and do some exercise. By the time I'd finished a 20-minute kettle bell workout, I'd forgotten all about how terrible my life had seemed. Life looked sweet again, and I got my teeth into the day with enthusiasm. My terrible life had been transformed, without my even noticing it.

So am I saying that when you're feeling down, you should do some exercise to change how you feel? No! There are no 'shoulds'. When we drift out of reality and into La-la Land, caught up in contaminated thinking, we lose touch with common sense and wisdom. The moment we fall out of contaminated thinking and into the present moment, the way forward is clear and the next step is obvious...

- Sometimes the next step is to press ahead with what we're doing.
- Sometimes the next step is to rest.
- Sometimes the next step is to do something different.
- Sometimes the next step is to wait for inspiration.

Authentic desires

Blaise Pascal famously wrote, 'The heart has its reasons, which reason does not know'. Authentic desires are results you want just because you want them. They may not even make rational sense, but they're authentic expressions of your being. Think about that for a moment...

> *Who you really are is the infinite intelligence and creative potential of life, the formless principles of* THOUGHT, CONSCIOUSNESS *and* MIND.
> *Your authentic desires are an expression of that infinite intelligence and creative potential.*
> *There is an intelligence and wisdom in you and your desires.*

Authentic desires often arrive as insights and realizations, though they may have been travelling with you for a while as a kind of 'knowing' at the back of your mind. Here are some of the questions I sometimes ask my clients to start pointing them in the direction of their authentic desires...

- What do you want? What would you like to have happen? What would you love to create or bring into being?

- How will you know you've got that result? What will you see, hear and feel that will let you know you've got it?

- If you could wave a magic wand and have everything the way you want it to be, what would that look like?

- What would you want if you knew you couldn't fail? What would you want if you knew it was OK to fail?

- What would you want if you were guaranteed to get it?

- What would you do if you had £100 million in the bank?

- What would you do if all work paid the same, and you could get whatever work you like?

- What would you want if you didn't have to do anything?

- What would you want if you knew you were going to be happy, secure, successful and loved, whether you got it or not?

- What would you want if you didn't have to be unhappy about not getting it?

- If there were a miracle tonight, and when you woke up tomorrow everything was the way you want it to be, how would you know a miracle had happened? What would you see, hear, feel and know that would let you know a miracle had taken place?

The purpose of these questions *isn't* for you to come up with specific goals as answers to them; the purpose is to guide you into a reflective space where you're more likely to have insights and realizations about what's important and meaningful to you and for you.

The power of commitment

When it comes to going on holiday, most people are 100% committed once they've booked their tickets. Once you know where you're going, the relevant goals are a practical matter (e.g. what to pack, when to get to the airport etc). It's the same with any result you want to create: commitment means (metaphorically) booking your ticket; making the decision that you're going to move in a certain direction/do something/make something happen/create something/bring something into being.

So should I *set* goals or not?

You *already* set and achieve goals. A more relevant question might be 'When is it useful for me to set goals?' The answer: when it makes sense. If it makes sense to set a specific target, set one. If it doesn't, don't. As stated earlier, goals can be useful for helping you set a direction, organize your own efforts or coordinate the efforts of a group of people. If you're creating a complex result that involves the work of many people, or things happening in a particular sequence, goals can be an incredibly useful part of the planning process (if you're building a house, you probably don't want the decorators arriving to start painting before the walls are up). But goals have no power in and of themselves. Set goals when it makes sense to do so. And if possible, set them from a clear state of mind.

When you've got nothing on your mind, you're free to give your best.

Practicality check: How is having a better understanding of goals going to help me get results?

CLARITY   plus   **ACTION**   equals   **RESULTS**

Figure 7.2: The CLARITY® Results Model

In Chapter 1, I introduced you to The CLARITY® Results Model, *Clarity plus Action equals Results*. Goals can be useful *tools* for prioritizing, co-ordinating and directing a variety of *actions*. The better you understand the tool (how you can use it, when to use it, when not to use it, etc) the more creative you can be with it.

So once you've got clarity about a result you want to create, how do you get into action?

Bottom line results: Most organizations rely on goals, targets and objectives to organize their efforts. This is a practical matter. But as soon as people believe their *psychological safety* is dependent on hitting the goal, they're at risk of creating a contaminated culture of stress, anxiety and unsustainable pressure. Of course, some goals are extremely important and can influence the very survival of an organization. The more you're able to approach goals from a place of clarity and common sense, the more likely you are to prevail.

---

keep exploring ⊹ connect with others
share your discoveries ⊹ deepen your understanding

Experiment: What are some of the results you'd love to create? What are some of the things you've been dreaming of? What possibilities would you love to breathe life into? You might like to take a few minutes to read the questions posed earlier in this chapter, and maybe even write down what occurs to you. Rather than being something you 'have to do', it can be fun to approach this from a place of reflection and curiosity. . .

www.jamiesmart.com/results7

8

Moving from Resistance to Action

....

Lots of people dream big and talk about big bold ideas but never do anything. I judge people by what they've done. The ratio of something to nothing is infinite. So just do something.

Peter Diamandis
Engineer, entrepreneur,
founder of the X Prize Foundation

'I'm scared... I'm not sure I want to go on the ride...'

My daughter Tallulah and I were standing in line, waiting for our turn to go on Air, a roller-coaster designed to simulate the experience of flying. We could hear the screams of the thrill-seekers on the ride as they looped skyward at high speed then plunged close to the ground, past fences, rocks and trees. Tallulah and I had been looking forward to this day for years – we'd had to wait until she was tall enough to go on the biggest, scariest rides – but as we stood in the queue, she was gripped by anxiety and having second thoughts. In the end, her desire for adventure won out, and we were soon locked into our harnesses, suspended in a 'Superman' position. The next two minutes were intoxicating as we dived, looped and swooped through the park, reaching speeds of 75 kilometres per hour. Tallulah loved it! When the ride was over, she said, 'I was really frightened in the queue, but the ride was amazing! I really enjoyed it'. Her statement stopped me in my tracks, and I asked her what she made of that. She said, 'I guess I was feeling my thinking in the queue, but I thought I was feeling the roller-coaster'.

Tallulah had seen through the oldest trick in the book, the mistaken belief that we're feeling something other than Thought in the moment. We're always living in the feeling of the principle of Thought, taking form in the moment. But it often seems as though we're feeling something other than Thought. Why? Because Thought is a trickster. It will point the finger at anything but itself. When she was in the queue, it seemed as though Tallulah's feelings were coming from her future roller-coaster ride. In fact, she was experiencing a Thought-generated illusion in the present. I told her, 'As you go through life, you will see countless examples of people who believe they're feeling the roller-coaster of their future, when really they're standing in the queue, feeling Thought in the moment'.

So what does this have to do with motivation, action and momentum? Here's what:

You don't need to feel motivated to take action.

In fact, it turns out that the most relevant time to take action can often be when you're *not* feeling motivated, enthusiastic or inspired. By the time you've finished this chapter, you're going to understand how to make progress on any project, no matter how motivated or unmotivated you feel, and no matter how uncomfortable or resistant you may have been with it until now. You're going to learn the art of making a start, no matter how big and scary your project may be.

Moods are like weather

I was having a conversation with a client who had a project she wanted to move forward with. She told me that sometimes she felt really inspired and motivated about the project, but that other days she felt uninspired and listless. The changes in her feeling about the project were confusing to her, and she was hesitant to take action and move forward. 'Would you want to make your project dependent on the weather?' I asked her. She replied that she wouldn't want that. 'Then why would you make your project dependent on how you feel on a given day?' She looked perplexed, and said she thought that if it was the right thing to do, she would always feel inspired about it. I said, 'Your feelings don't know about your project; your feelings only know about THOUGHT in the moment. Your moods are like the weather; they don't mean anything'. I explained that while purpose and inspiration can give you a glimpse of a possible future, we're always going to be subject to the ebb and flow of THOUGHT in the moment. And like the weather, your moods are not a reliable foundation to base your future on.

DISTINCTION: The inspiration myth vs the perspiration reality

The inventor Thomas Edison famously described genius as 'one percent inspiration, ninety-nine percent perspiration'. The **inspiration myth** goes something like this: 'I'll start taking action *once* I'm feeling inspired.

Then I'll have a crystal clear vision of what I want to create, and I'll know *exactly* how I'm going to do it. My feeling of inspiration will give me the motivation I need to put in the effort'.

While acts of creation *sometimes* result from this kind of inspiration, it's the exception rather than the rule. A much more common and reliable pattern of creation is the **perspiration reality**: 'I'm not feeling inspired, but I'll start taking action anyway. At some point, inspiration strikes, or it doesn't. Either way, I'll keep taking action because what I'm working on matters to me'.

In January 2003, I decided to write an article a week and share it with the people I was connected with. I knew I wanted to share what I was learning, but I'd never written an article before, and I definitely *wasn't* feeling inspired. In fact, I was feeling afraid of being judged and criticized. I wrote my first article and shared it with the people in my email address book. I continued to write an article every week for the next eight years, by which point I had over 80,000 subscribers reading my posts. Sometimes I'd get struck by inspiration and an article would pour out of me, but more often the articles were a result of the 'perspiration' approach.

The problem with the inspiration myth is that it can keep people stuck in passivity, waiting for metaphorical lightning to strike so they can start moving forward.

The power of passivity

'Right! So you're saying I should *never* be passive. That I have to take action no matter how I'm feeling?' No, I'm not saying that. Passivity can actually be a source of power and inspiration, something you can get to work *for* you rather than against you. Many of the great discoveries through history have come as the result of a realization: fresh new thinking that showed up when the thinker's state of mind was one of contemplation, reflection or meditation. So how does this reconcile with the 'perspiration reality'? Many of my clients appreciate The *CLARITY*® *Productivity Quadrant*:

Figure 8.1:   The CLARITY® Productivity Quadrant

The quadrant describes four zones:

1.   The Zone of Resistance (*passive*)

We all oscillate between periods of clarity and times when we get caught up in our thinking. When we're caught up, it's almost always an example of contaminated thinking, the mistaken belief that our feelings are coming from somewhere *other than* THOUGHT in the moment. The *Zone of Resistance* isn't much fun. Nevertheless, we all end up there from time to time. We have seasons, just like the rest of nature. We're not all 100% productive 100% of the time. You might like to reflect on the question, 'Where do I believe my experience is coming from?' When we're in the *Zone of Resistance*, it almost always seems like our feelings are letting us know about the future, the past, our circumstances, other people or ourselves. Alternatively, you can jump into *uninspired* action.

2. The Zone of Uninspired Action (*active*)

Don't just sit there; do something! The *Zone of Uninspired Action* often accounts for the 'perspiration reality' we explored earlier. Getting into action gives you something to be doing and focusing on. Your mind is a self-correcting system, so you're going to get fresh new thinking/feeling eventually. When you're taking action, it's surprising how often new thinking shows up. When a person's in the *Zone of Uninspired Action*, there's sometimes a sense of strain, struggle and 'slogging away at it'. That's OK; as my dear friend and colleague Garret Kramer says, 'Stay in the game'. You may even find yourself pausing and easing into a *reflective* state of mind.

3. The Zone of Reflection (*passive*)

Don't just do something; sit there! The *Zone of Reflection* is a powerful source of fresh new thinking, a zone of renewal and regeneration. Newton's theory of universal gravitation, Archimedes' eureka moment and Steve Jobs' insights about the future of the music business all came in moments of reflection, when they weren't actively thinking about the matter at hand. There are countless contexts where people enter a reflective and contemplative state of mind. I've had numerous examples from clients over the years (including walking, sitting by the ocean, riding, meditating, reading, listening to certain music, sitting in the bath). As you get a deeper understanding of the principles behind clarity, you'll find yourself being guided into the *Zone of Reflection* more easily and spontaneously. And from time to time, you'll get struck with inspiration, an insight that shows you the way forward. When that happens, it's time for *inspired* action.

4. The Zone of Inspired Action (*active*)

The *Zone of Inspired Action* is where you can't seem to put a foot wrong; where everything's falling into place and you feel guided and directed. Enjoy it when it comes, and stay in the game when it doesn't. Even when it's nowhere to be found, you can relax in the knowledge that it's only ever a thought away.

The power of the pause

There's an old tale about anthropologists studying a tribe of Aboriginal Australians on walkabout. The tribesmen would walk or run, sometimes for hours, then suddenly stop completely still. Sometimes they would run for an hour then stop for a few minutes. Then, they would run for only a few minutes, followed by an hour's pause. Running, walking, pausing... They concocted theories and explanations, but the anthropologists were unable to discern any kind of pattern they could use to predict when the Aboriginal people would move and when they would be still. Finally, the anthropologists approached one of the elders to ask the purpose of these mysterious pauses. 'We're waiting for our souls to catch up to us', the elder replied.

The art of making things happen

Do something...

> *When you take action, you can discover things that you're unlikely to stumble upon in the privacy of your own head... You put your theories and ideas about life to the test, and get direct feedback from an impartial agent: reality!*

As you get a deeper understanding of the principles behind clarity, you'll find yourself with a stronger foundation for the action you take. You'll become more attuned to your own rhythms, knowing when to act and when to pause for reflection. As you keep waking up to the power of wisdom and intuition, you'll come to rely more and more on them as a source of insight, guidance and realization.

CLARITY   plus   **ACTION**   equals   **RESULTS**

Figure 8.2: The CLARITY® Results Model

Practicality check: How is moving from resistance to action going to help me get results?

- As your understanding of the principles behind clarity continues to deepen, you'll find that you have a stronger foundation for the action you take.

- You'll become more attuned to your own rhythms, knowing when to act and when to pause for reflection.

- As you keep waking up to the power of wisdom and intuition, you'll come to rely more and more on them as a source of insight, guidance and realization.

- When you take action, you can discover things that you're unlikely to figure out in the privacy of your own head.

- When you take action, you put your theories and ideas about life to the test. You get direct feedback from an impartial agent: reality!

So as your personal transformation continues, it's time to jump into your *interpersonal* transformation, a domain that will give you plenty of opportunity for connection, experimentation and action.

Bottom line results: In a world awash with 'productivity systems', it can be a relief to realize that you possess a *built-in* productivity system that is tailor-made for you, and the situations you find yourself in. As you get more in tune with your own rhythms, and continue deepening your understanding of these principles, you'll find this having an enormous impact on your ability to create results.

---

keep exploring ⁂ connect with others
share your discoveries ⁂ deepen your understanding

Experiment: Is there something you've been struggling to bring into being until now? Perhaps it's something you'd love to make happen, but you don't know where to start. What's a next step you could take? What's something you could do without having to feel even slightly motivated to do it? Just for fun, make a start, just to see what happens. . .

www.jamiesmart.com/results8

PART TWO

IMPACT
Your Interpersonal Transformation

Everything about us – our brains, our minds and our bodies – is geared towards collaboration in social systems. This is our most powerful survival strategy, the key to our success as a species, and it is precisely this that breaks down in most forms of mental suffering.

Bessel van der Kolk
Psychiatrist, PTSD researcher

We cannot live for ourselves alone. Our lives are connected by a thousand invisible threads, and along these sympathetic fibers, our actions run as causes and return to us as results.

Herman Melville
Novelist, teacher, sailor, poet

9

The Principles of Impact

Everyone needs a coach.

Bill Gates
Co-founder of Microsoft, entrepreneur, philanthropist

'Would you like me to collaborate with you on growing your business?'

Pete Bryceland responded to my message minutes after I'd sent it. 'Yes I would!' As our conversation unfolded, he revealed that he'd been making a living as a transformation professional (he'd earned a little less than £20,000 that year, coaching people) but was finding it challenging. He wanted to earn significantly more money, enjoy the process more, and feel greater freedom. It emerged that Pete loved coaching, and got great results with his clients, but found charging by the hour frustrating and difficult. He wanted to move to a high-value coaching package model so he could have more committed clients, increase his income and stabilize his cash flow.

But there was a problem: Pete hated selling.

I invited Pete to join the beta-test group for a new programme I was developing, and ended up coaching him in front of a live audience a few weeks later. He explained that when he had conversations with potential clients, they were excited about working with him, but as soon as they started asking about what it would cost, Pete became awkward, disconnected and tongue-tied. He'd lost three sales in the previous few weeks due to this 'selling-anxiety'. As we talked, Pete started becoming more reflective, and a sense of connection started developing between us. About 20 minutes into the conversation, Pete had a realization, and started to see the situation differently. He got in touch with me a month later to let me know that he'd signed up two clients on packages of £10,000 each since our coaching conversation. He'd made more money as a result of that one insight than he had in the previous year!

Many of the greatest performers on the planet have coaches. From golfer Rory McIlroy to Google CEO Eric Schmidt; from pop diva Beyonce to surgeon Atul Gawande. Why? Because the perspective, understanding and mindset of an impactful coach can unlock your potential and bring out your best performance. A truly transformational coach is able to speak to a person's deepest wisdom and their highest inspiration. They're influential, wise and impactful enough to call forth profound changes and extraordinary results from others.

And what does this have to do with the principles of impact?

It turns out that you can realize the leverage points the world's most transformational coaches use to create massive impact; in your own life, and in the lives of others. You see, the principles of impact apply in every situation, whether you're giving a speech or out on a first date; whether you're parenting your teenager or applying for a job. The principles of impact apply in the domains of leadership, management, performance, innovation, friendship, parenting, public speaking, selling, negotiating and even dating.

The CLARITY® Impact Model

You know those days where you can't put a foot wrong… When everything falls into place, you get the ideas you need exactly when you need them, and you finish the day feeling productive and fulfilled… And then there are those *other* days, when it really seems like you would have been better just to *stay* in bed… The days when everything seems like a chore, and it's tough to find your groove. The difference between those two days is the state of mind you're in… your level of clarity. Your level of clarity determines how you're showing up in the world, and the impact you're going to have. The *CLARITY® Impact Model* is a simple way of relating to your innate capacity for learning, changing, growing, communicating and getting results. It applies equally to individuals, 1:1 relationships and groups. You can think of it as a metaphor that points to the principles behind clarity and your innate capacity for having an impact. It consists of the following elements:

1   Clarity of connection

2   Clarity of thought

3   Clarity of understanding

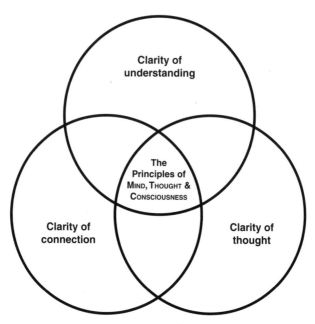

Figure 9.1: The CLARITY® Impact Model

You're going to get an overview of these three kinds of clarity in this chapter, then we'll be exploring each of them more deeply in the chapters that follow.

1. Clarity of connection

Once again: human beings have a more highly evolved capacity for connection and relationship than any other species. Social groups are a big part of the reality we're built for. The feeling of connection can be a powerful communicator of trust and credibility when it comes to persuasion, influence and leadership. In more intimate relationships, the feeling of love and connection is the rich soil that feeds the roots of the relationship and allows it to grow and evolve. We all have times when we're feeling connected; connected to another person... connected to our true selves... connected to life as a whole. We also have times when we feel less connected, or even isolated. When you're feeling connected, there's a sense of closeness and intimacy that carries its own credibility. When we're hanging out in

La-la Land, caught up in contaminated thinking, we lose that sense of connection. The moment you fall out of contaminated thinking and into the reality of the moment, your sense of connection re-emerges.

2. Clarity of thought

Clarity of thought is a predictor of high performance, valuable insights and impactful communications. Unsurprisingly, clarity of thought is also correlated with a deeper sense of connection. When you've got a clear mind, you're free to give your best, whatever the context. We all have times when we're clear-headed, present and available to the moment. We also have times when we're preoccupied, with a lot on our minds. Clarity of thought is the variable that determines where on that spectrum you're showing up. When we're caught up in contaminated thinking, our clarity of thought is low. The moment you wake up from the outside-in misunderstanding, clarity of thought returns.

3. Clarity of understanding

Every person on the planet has their own understanding of how life works. In some areas of life, your embodied understanding is closely aligned with reality, and you get good results. In other areas of life, your embodied understanding is adrift from reality, and you struggle. The greater your awareness of the inside-out nature of the mind, the greater your clarity of understanding is. And here's the thing: we all have times when we feel connected; we all have times when we have clarity of thought. But your clarity of understanding is the ultimate leverage point for increasing the amount of time you spend clear-headed and feeling connected. When you *do* get caught up in contaminated thinking, your clarity of understanding determines how quickly your mind will self-correct.

The principles of impact

The *CLARITY*® *Impact Model* is poly-contextual; it's relevant in any domain that involves people. When I'm teaching coaches, I refer to it as the *CLARITY*® *Coaching Model*. In leadership workshops, it becomes the *CLARITY® Leadership Model*. The same goes for parenting, teaching, public speaking, influence and relationships. The reason this model applies across all contexts is simple...

> *The principles behind clarity are at play in every*
> *human interaction...*
> *If a person is having an experience, it's being created by the*
> *principles of* MIND, THOUGHT *and* CONSCIOUSNESS.

It's liberating to realize that *you're already connected* to the principles of impact. The principles of MIND, THOUGHT and CONSCIOUSNESS are creating your experience *right now*, in this very moment. As you deepen your understanding of the nature of these principles, you'll increase your ability to have an impact with others and create meaningful results.

Exceptional productivity

Mamoon Yusaf reached out to me because he was considering coming on my annual life transformation retreat. We arranged a time to speak so I could find out if he was a good fit for the retreat, and vice versa. During that conversation, Mamoon mentioned that he was struggling over a painful separation he'd been through nine months earlier. He was running a successful business, but beating himself up about the relationship was having a negative impact on his clarity, wellbeing and productivity. During our conversation, Mamoon had a profound and liberating insight. He later wrote, 'Over the following two weeks, I had a totally clear head and was exceptionally productive with meeting deadlines. I didn't realize until much later that the coaching call with Jamie talking about relationships actually undid habitual thinking patterns and deep-rooted limiting beliefs that had been seriously sabotaging all areas of my life'.

Mamoon's realization resulted in an increased clarity of understanding. His embodied understanding of his mind and emotions became more closely aligned with the one way the mind always works. This 'jump in consciousness' had a *subtractive* effect, clearing his mind of much of the contaminated thinking which had been holding him back. A few weeks later, he joined me on the retreat, and his understanding of these principles now forms the basis of his work as a transformational coach in the Muslim community.

Practicality check: How are the principles of impact going to help me get results?

- You've *already* been using the principles of impact to get the results you've created so far in your life, whether you've realized it or not.

- The principles of impact are a *description* of what's behind high performance, connection and creativity, not a *prescription* or 'how-to' model.

- When you've got nothing on your mind, you're free to give your best.

- A deeper understanding of the principles behind clarity will help you experience a clear mind and deeper connections more frequently.

- As you learn to navigate using these principles, you'll start experiencing the inevitable results of becoming more closely aligned with reality, including richer relationships, effortless influence and increased creativity.

Transformational results

I conducted a case-study interview with Pete Bryceland a year after he joined my programme to document what the impact of this understanding had been for him. Pete's results have been transformational. He now feels a sense of ease and enjoyment about clients, money and selling. Pete coaches business owners, executives and managers who are feeling overwhelmed and under constant pressure to perform. He says, 'If I want more money, I just go out and get it'. He's increased his income significantly, but he said the *biggest* impact has been the sense of freedom and security he now feels. This has meant he's been able to spend more time with his family (one of the main reasons he decided to set up his own business in the first place).

My transformational conversations with Pete and Mamoon each started with a deep sense of connection. So how can you start experiencing that kind of connection to help you create the results that matter to you?

Bottom line results: You can use the leverage points discovered by great coaches to create massive impact in your own life, and in the lives of others. Every business relies on people – colleagues, clients, stakeholders, suppliers – to get results. The *CLARITY® Impact Model* explains how the principles behind clarity play out in every human situation. As you experiment with these principles, you're going to find yourself enjoying your interactions more, and having a more positive effect on others, with predictably positive results.

| **CLARITY** | plus | **ACTION** | equals | **RESULTS** |

Figure 9.2: The CLARITY® Results Model

keep exploring ⁜ connect with others
share your discoveries ⁜ deepen your understanding

Experiment: Start to notice the places and situations in your life where you're already having an impact. Where are you already doing well? What areas have been falling short until now? Reflect on the effect your state of mind has been having either to constrain or amplify your impact. Where would you like to be having an even greater impact?

www.jamiesmart.com/results9

10

The Secret of Powerful Connection

No man is an island, entire of itself; every man is a piece of the continent.

John Donne
Poet, priest, lawyer

'I knew I shouldn't have come here. I'm booking a flight home...'

My girlfriend and I had arrived in Maui the night before, and she'd been intoxicated by the beautiful scents, warm breeze and tropical vibe. We'd been feeling close and connected, but the next morning she was cold, panicked and distant. She said, 'I don't like it. Hawaii's not what I expected. I knew I shouldn't have come here. I'm booking a flight home'.

I could see exactly what was going on. She was feeling agitated and uncomfortable. Her feelings were letting her know about THOUGHT in the moment, but she mistakenly believed they were letting her know about Maui. I flew into damage-limitation mode. 'Let's go for coffee and you can sort out flights at the cafe'. I was sure that, by the time we'd driven to the coffee shop, the sight of long sandy beaches, surfers and swaying palm trees would have changed her mind.

But I was wrong. As the minutes passed, her mood grew worse and she started blaming me for it. 'I knew this was a mistake. Why did I listen to you? This is what always happens'. Now I was starting to get annoyed. *I love Maui. Why couldn't she see how amazing it was? What was I doing here with this moody woman? I hope she does get a flight home so I can relax and enjoy this exotic corner of paradise.* By this time I was feeling angry, frustrated and disconnected. And that's when the voice of wisdom whispered in my ear...

'Where do you believe your feelings are coming from? Do you think they're letting you know about her?'

The realization hit me in a flash. I'd been doing *exactly* the same thing *she* was. My girlfriend had been feeling THOUGHT in the moment, but she'd been blaming those feelings on Maui. I'd been feeling THOUGHT in the moment, but I'd been blaming those feelings on my girlfriend. The feelings of peace, humility and connection came rushing back to me as I fell out of contaminated thinking and into the moment. I was struck with a sense of awe and respect for the compelling nature of the outside-in deception, and the wisdom and intelligence of the principles behind clarity. I'd fallen out of the illusion of disconnection and landed in the fact of connection. You see...

You're always connected, to everything and everyone...
Whether you realize it or not...

My heart went out to her. She was a long way from home, and she was feeling insecure. She was caught up in an illusion that had been fooling me too until just moments before. My position of judgement and justified anger had been replaced with love and compassion. I didn't say anything, but I could see her innocence in the face of the outside-in misunderstanding. A moment later, she fell out of it too. 'Don't mind me, I'm just being silly'. The storm which had been threatening to destroy our holiday had passed, and the sunshine of clarity and connection had emerged.

We all live and work in a matrix of relationships, and in one way or another, many of our results are reliant on other people. As technology makes our world more tangibly connected, social and emotional intelligence are becoming more important than ever. The experience of connection is like 'WD40' for impactful relationships. By the time you've finished this chapter, you'll understand where the experience of connection comes from, what gets in the way of it, and how to experience effortless connection more of the time, in the situations where it matters.

Where does connection come from?

We've each had the experience (even if only occasionally) of feeling deeply connected with ourselves, with another person and even with life itself. And everyone's had the experience (even if only occasionally) of feeling isolated, disconnected and alone. Both of these polarities are universal aspects of the human experience, and an understanding of them is incredibly powerful when it comes to relationships. To understand where connection comes from, we're going to be drawing a distinction between the *experience* of connection and the *fact* of connection:

DISTINCTION: The fact of connection vs the experience of connection

In his fascinating video, *A Universe From Nothing*, cosmologist Lawrence Krauss gives a brilliant, eloquent and elegant proof that the universe has arisen from nothing; from a sea of formless energy. The fact is that we're each made of the 'nothingness' from which the universe sprang. On one level, we can experience ourselves as separate from each other, and distinct from our physical environment. This is a practical matter. But on another level, we are all made of this same formless energy. Like waves in an ocean, we are all part of the same undivided wholeness. Just as waves don't leave the ocean and 'go solo', we are never disconnected from this infinite ocean of energy. This is **the fact of connection**.

The experience of connection is often described as a feeling of love and closeness combined with rapport. People sometimes say 'we just clicked' or describe themselves as being on the same wavelength.

> *The felt experience of connection is an expression of*
> *the fact of connection...*
> *You become aware of it when there's nothing getting in the way.*

The thing that tends to *get* in the way is contaminated thinking arising from the outside-in misunderstanding. The experience of connection rapidly evaporates when we lose ourselves in contaminated thinking. But the moment we insightfully see the inside-out nature of life, we fall out of our contaminated thinking and wake up to reality. As we return to the present moment, we find ourselves back in the experience of connection with our true nature, with other people, and with life as a whole.

A sense of connection is the 'transformation superhighway' when it comes to impact. When you're in the experience of connection...

- You 'carry your credibility', giving the other person a powerful and unique experience of who they really are.

- You make it easier for people both to *like* you and to find commonalities with you, increasing your influence.

- You can impact a person or group deeply, with each of you being guided by wisdom.

- You're more available to insight; fresh new thinking that can help you and the people you're impacting.

- You can drop your agenda and allow the conversation to unfold, increasing your credibility in the process.

- You're in the space for genuine transformation.

The experience of connection is natural when there's nothing else in the way. But **the fact of connection** is constant, even when you're not aware of it. And here's the great thing: as you insightfully realize connection as a pre-existing *fact*, the *experience* of connection becomes deeper and more frequent.

IMPLICATION: Separate realities

Remember: your feelings are giving you feedback about the 'glasses' you're wearing, not who or what you're looking at. How you perceive other people is always consistent with *your own* level of clarity in the moment...

- When you're feeling frustrated, other people often appear to be the source of that frustration.

- When you're feeling appreciative, other people may appear to be a source of blessings.

- When you're feeling angry, the chances of another person seeming like the source of that anger are pretty high.

We each live in a separate, THOUGHT-generated perceptual reality. We're living in a THOUGHT-generated experience, but it often *seems* as though our feelings are letting us know about something *other than* THOUGHT. In fact, it often seems as though our feelings are telling us about another person. But that's not possible, at the level of principle. Your feelings are letting you know about what's happening in *your perception*.

The CLARITY® Relationship Quadrant provides a simple way of understanding this...

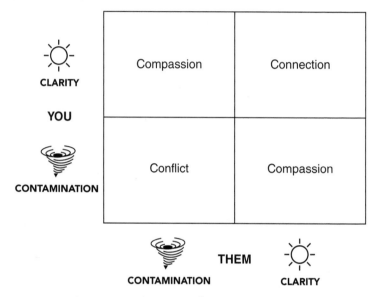

Figure 10.1:   The CLARITY® Relationship Quadrant

1.   The Zone of Conflict

Bob and Jane feel angry at each other. Their angry feelings are letting each of them know they're wearing their angry-goggles; that THOUGHT in the moment is taking an angry form. But each of them *mistakenly* believes their feelings are telling them about the other person. They're in *The Zone of Conflict*.

2.   The Zone of Connection

Bob and Jane have a big shouting match, followed by passionate make-up sex. In the heat of the moment, their heads clear, and they start feeling deeply connected to each other.

3.   The Zone of Compassion (1)

Later on, Bob starts getting upset again, but Jane still feels connected and clear-headed. She sees that Bob has just lost his bearings, and her heart goes out to him, full of compassion.

4. The Zone of Compassion (2)

The next day, Bob wakes up with a clear head. He goes to Jane to apologize for his hasty words the night before, but she's in a rush to get out the door and snaps at him. He sees that Jane has lost her bearings. He feels compassion for her, seeing the innocence in the ebb and flow of her thinking.

The CLARITY® Relationship Quadrant is very simple. It works on the basis that:

- Your feelings are always letting you know about THOUGHT taking form in your experience, moment to moment.

- That other people will appear to be consistent with *your* THOUGHT-generated perceptual reality.

- That when neither participant has clarity, it's a recipe for conflict.

- That when *one* person in a relationship has clarity, it creates space for the other person to start finding clarity too.

This is incredibly encouraging news; it means that clarity in your relationships starts with you.

Practicality check: How is connection going to help me get results?

- The feeling of connection is an essential nutrient for interpersonal relationships, including (but not limited to) colleagues, employees, bosses, clients, tribe members, audiences, suppliers, friends, family, lovers and strangers.

- When people feel connected to you, they experience you as honest, authentic and transparent.

- When you're feeling connected to your true self and to life, you're more open to insights, realizations and innovative thinking.

- When it comes to impacting another person, the feeling of connection creates a space where genuine communication can take place, and transformation can occur.

After our rocky start, my girlfriend and I ended up having a wonderful result: we shared three weeks in Maui, and enjoyed plenty of fun, adventure and connection. While we've since gone out separate ways, we both look back on it as one of our favourite adventures together. When your head clears and you fall out of La-la Land, you discover that you have what you need in the moment. So how can you learn to rely on that clarity emerging when and where you need it?

Bottom line results: A sense of connection is the 'transformation super-highway' for impact. One of the simplest ways to get the benefits of connection is by listening deeply to the person or people you're with. Many people don't so much listen as 'wait for their turn to speak', but people can tell when they've got 100% of your attention. Listening and connection can turn a previously unproductive meeting into a source of fresh new insights and innovative solutions, deepening relationships in the process.

---

keep exploring ❖ connect with others
share your discoveries ❖ deepen your understanding

Experiment: In any conversations you have this week, notice the ebb and flow of the feeling of connection. If you want to increase the sense of connection, experiment with listening to the person with 'nothing on your mind'. Most people listen with a lot on their mind. They're thinking about what they're going to say next, trying to figure out what question to ask, almost like they're waiting for 'their turn to speak'. But that isn't listening. When you truly listen, you allow yourself to be present to the other person, bathing them in your attention. Experiment with this, and notice how it's different.

www.jamiesmart.com/results10

11

The Source of Superb Performance

....

I saw the angel in the marble and carved until I set him free.

Michelangelo
Sculptor, painter, architect

'If you think too much about a race you just make yourself more nervous...'

The sprinter, Olympic Gold-medal winner Usain Bolt is currently regarded as the fastest man on earth. Before the race, while his competitors are running through complex pre-race routines, visualizing their victories and performing various rituals, Bolt fools around and chats with the crowd. When asked why he favours this approach, he said 'I've learned over the years that if you think too much about a race you just make yourself more nervous'. Bolt's goal on the day is obvious – he's unlikely to forget that he wants to cross the finish line. Once you know where you're headed, clarity is your best ally for helping you get there. So why is it that some people produce world-class performances over and over again, while others struggle when the heat is on?

High performance leads to superb results

People give their best performances when they've got nothing on their mind. When your mind is clear, you're available to the moment, connected to your innate source of guidance, resilience and creativity. Whether you're an artist or an athlete... a transformation professional or a knowledge-worker... a parent or a public-speaker... a fighter or a lover... your best results are a function of the quality of your performance in the moment. And where does high performance come from? Your state of mind.

How your state of mind affects your performance

In their December 2014 *Harvard Business Review* article, 'How Your State of Mind Affects Your Performance', researchers Andrew Caillet, Jeremy Hirshberg and Stefano Petti reported their findings from a survey of 740 leaders internationally. The aim of the survey was to determine the impact of the leaders' state of mind on their performance and effectiveness, and to discover what they did to manage those states. The researchers identified 18 states of mind, ranging from 'depressed', 'hopeless' and 'desperate' to 'elated', 'ecstatic' and 'euphoric'. 94% of the leaders identified the states that drove the highest levels of performance as 'calm', 'happy' and 'energized' (CHE). At the other end of the spectrum, leaders admitted to spending a certain amount of time in low-performance states; 'frustrated', 'anxious', 'tired' and 'stressed' (FATS). The article suggested that CHE states not only drove high performance; these states also seemed to be 'transmitted' to other people. Conversely, the FATS states often delivered *short-term* results, but were damaging in the long term, particularly in the domain of relationships. Leaders also said that when the FATS states were 'consistently present in the organizational culture or environment', they found them difficult to change.

CLARITY   equals   **CAPACITY**   minus   **CONTAMINATION**

Figure 11.1:   The CLARITY® Equation

When we struggle with frustration, anxiety and stress, we've been hijacked by contaminated thinking. Think about it: if you tell someone you're frustrated, stressed or worried, the first thing they typically do is ask you, 'Why? What about?' These questions innocently affirm the outside-in misunderstanding by inviting you to attribute your feelings to something *other than* THOUGHT in the moment. The CHE states, on the other hand, are natural for us when our minds are *free* from contaminated thinking. Many people have described these CHE states by different names. Psychologist Mihaly Csikszentmihalyi describes it as 'flow'; athletes talk about being 'in the zone'; musicians call it 'the groove'; I call it 'clarity of thought'. And here's the thing…

Peace, connection and clarity are your nature…
Just as the sun is always at the centre of the solar system…
Even when clouds are preventing you from seeing it…
Peace, connection and clarity are at the core of your being…
Even when contaminated thinking is preventing you from
experiencing it.

State control: correlation does not imply causation

Having established the link between state of mind, performance and results, Caillet, Hirshberg and Petti then ask 'How do leaders shift from lower states of mind to higher states of mind and improve their effectiveness and performance?' As you'll understand, this question invites leaders to look *away* from the mind's self-clearing capacity, and *misattribute* the power to things in the (neutral) world of form (if the leaders had been asked for the cause of the FATS states, we would see a similar misattribution).

Unsurprisingly, the executives identified a variety of additive approaches, including visualization, positive thoughts, deep breathing, listening to music, exercise, a healthy diet and adequate sleep. While it would be foolish to argue against the value of exercise, a healthy diet or adequate sleep, this is a classic case of confusing *correlation* with *causation*. A person's thoughts, states, words and behaviour are consistent with their level of consciousness/clarity of understanding. A person who's operating at a higher level of consciousness will tend to spend more time in CHE states, and make healthier choices in general. While there can certainly be the appearance of a 'virtuous circle' quality in this, the idea that the states are caused by (or hampered by) external factors is fundamentally untrue.

Reality check

'But doesn't meditation lead to changes in brain structure?' Yes and no. Recent research suggests that the brains of experienced meditators are different from those of non-meditators. It even suggests that eight weeks of meditation practice can make a difference to subjects' brains; however, this looks like another case of correlation being taken for causation. The purpose of the *act of meditating* is to guide a person into a *state of meditation*. There are many times that people enter a state of meditation, including walking, fishing, bathing, listening to music or sitting in the park. The state of meditation is a natural function of the human mind; it is not caused by the act of meditating. It looks likely that experiencing the *state of meditation* can lead to changes in brain structure, regardless of how, when or where that state is entered. (My team and I are in the process of designing a research project to test this hypothesis.)

So if methods, techniques and practices are not the answer, what is?

The only thing you need for a high-performance state of mind

Think of one of your favourite films or TV shows. There are two things you need to enjoy the show:

You have to be able to be 'swept away' by the film

The best directors are masters of creating an illusionary reality. They use sound and light to create a La-la Land: an *imaginary* world that we experience as though it's an *actual* reality. When we get 'swept away' by a movie, we get drawn into the director's illusionary world and experience it as real. We temporarily 'forget' that the characters and events we're experiencing are light and shadows on a screen. We get drawn into the director's illusionary world, and relate to the characters and events as though they're really happening. When someone *doesn't* get swept away by a film, you'll hear them say something like, 'I couldn't buy it' or 'I couldn't get into it'. They weren't 'fooled' by the illusionary reality, so couldn't suspend their disbelief and enter into the director's La-la Land.

You have to be able to 'wake up' from the film's illusionary reality

While it's wonderful to be swept away by a film, we also have to be able to wake up to the fact that it's an illusion (otherwise you'd phone the fire department if flames appeared on the screen). Our ability to fall out of the director's La-la Land is a function of our understanding of the *nature* of movies. You developed this understanding at a very early age and today, your ability to 'wake up' from the film is automatic. Of course, little children don't yet understand the nature of film – that's why it's important to be selective about what they watch. Telling a child who doesn't understand the nature of film that 'it's just a movie' has no effect. It's your embodied understanding that allows you to wake up from the illusion and return to reality. Of course, you never actually left reality; you just *thought* you did.

Enjoying a movie requires an oscillation between these two positions; being swept away by the film's illusionary reality, occasionally punctuated by waking up to the fact that it's just a movie. This is exactly the same kind of oscillation you need to enjoy your life, to wake up from FATS and experience CHE states of mind, more and more of the time.

You have to be able to be 'swept away' by the principle of THOUGHT

The principle of THOUGHT is the best film director in the world. It creates a multi-sensory illusionary reality that we bring to life using the principle of CONSCIOUSNESS and experience as real. When we're moved by the sight of a beautiful sunrise, filled up with love for someone we care about or inspired by a leader's visionary words, we've been swept away by the principle of THOUGHT. Those *beautiful* feelings are coming from THOUGHT taking form in the moment within you, but it often *seems* like they're coming from the sunrise, the leader or the loved one. When we're anxious about a future appointment, worried about someone we care about or angry about someone's past behaviours, we've been swept away by the principle of THOUGHT. Those *uncomfortable* feelings are coming from THOUGHT taking form in the moment, but it *seems* like they're coming from somewhere *other than* THOUGHT; from the appointment, the person we're concerned about or the wrongdoer's behaviours. This is the illusionary power of THOUGHT.

You have to be able to 'wake up' from THOUGHT's illusory reality

We all get swept away by THOUGHT, but we all have the power to wake up from THOUGHT's illusory reality; to fall out of the La-La Land of our contaminated thinking, and fall present to the moment. We've all had the experience of being very worried about something before going to sleep, then waking up the next morning wondering how we'd managed to get so bothered about it. Little children intuitively grasp the illusory nature of THOUGHT, able to flit from sobbing with misery to giggling with joy in the blink of an eye. In any moment, we can *realize* that we're feeling THOUGHT taking form, and *not* what we're thinking about. The instant this happens, we fall out of the La-la Land of our misunderstanding, and 'fall awake' to the present.

A rich, enjoyable experience of life relies on an oscillation between the two positions mentioned above; getting swept away by the principle of THOUGHT in the moment, then waking up to the illusory nature of THOUGHT. And as you continue to explore the principles behind clarity, your understanding of the deceptive and illusory nature of THOUGHT will allow you to enjoy this oscillation more and more. And it turns out that's the only thing you need to live a life you love and experience high-performance states of mind, more of the time.

The one thing you need to enjoy a movie is an understanding of the nature of film.
The one thing you need to enjoy your life is an understanding of the nature of THOUGHT.

So what is the nature of THOUGHT?

In Chapter 5, I introduced you to cognitive neuroscientist Donald Hoffman's 'interface theory' of perception. Once again, we can think of time and space as our desktop, and the various 'objects' in our world as symbols or icons on that desktop. You can think of the principle of THOUGHT as being like the 'pixels' of our perception; the creative energy that 'renders' the desktop (space and time), as well as the objects we perceive on that desktop (e.g. people, places, things, our own bodies, our self-images, the countless thoughts that pass through our minds each day). The principle of CONSCIOUSNESS is like the computer's screen, giving you an *experience* of the THOUGHT-generated reality you're creating in the moment. All of this is powered by the principle of MIND, the intelligent energy behind life. The formless principles behind clarity are at your very core; the essence of your being…

You were born into the principle of THOUGHT *just as you were born into the principle of gravity.*
You're living in a THOUGHT*-generated perceptual reality and experiencing it as an actual reality.*

And remember; you're *built* for reality; you're optimized for results. The CLARITY® model is subtractive; as your understanding of these principles continues to deepen, it takes things *off* your mind, giving you *less* to think about.

Practicality check: How is a clear mind going to help me get results?

People get their best ideas and deliver their best performances when they've got nothing on their mind. As you translate insights into action, you create results.

| CLARITY | plus | ACTION | equals | RESULTS |

Figure 11.2:   The CLARITY® Results Model

We started this chapter with Usain Bolt explaining how he avoids over-thinking prior to a race; that he'll have what he needs when he needs it. He went on to say, 'My mind automatically turns on to what I have got to do when I need it to. So, when I'm in the blocks, it switches on. I say to myself, "I gotta run now – let's do this". And everything I have worked on for so long just comes together'.

So what enables a person to have such a high level of confidence in and reliance on the mind's self-clearing ability, and all the other innate capacities for creating results?

Bottom line results: Clarity of understanding drives 'high-performance' states of mind. High-performance states of mind drive results. People 'pick up on' each other's states of mind, so you're in a highly leveraged position to have a significant impact on everyone you come into contact with.

NB: Both high-performance and low-performance states of mind are highly contagious. Act accordingly.

---

keep exploring ❖ connect with others
share your discoveries ❖ deepen your understanding

Experiment: Start to pay attention to what people say after they've delivered an outstanding performance. Contrast this to what they say after they've delivered a poor performance. What do they attribute their results to? An easy source of examples is sports performance. Commentators will almost always attribute performances (good and bad) to external factors. Competitors will often attribute poor performances to external factors. But when they're playing well, notice how their explanations change. And what about you? What are some of the times or situations when you perform at your best? What is your experience of that?

www.jamiesmart.com/results11

12

The Catalyst for Transformational Results

....

The difficulty's not getting new ideas; new ideas are cheap. I mean there are plenty of new ideas. It's getting rid of the old ideas; that's the hard part.

Carlo Rovelli
Physicist, author

'How are you going to prepare? What plans have you made?'

Ankush Jain (one of my apprentices) was due to be observing during a three-day coaching intensive with a new client, and he wanted to know my plans for the session. The intensive is an in-depth, one-to-one experience designed to significantly increase the client's embodied understanding of life and establish a new 'platform' for living. We'd already had two phone calls with Ani (the client) to get clear on what a successful outcome would be from his perspective, so I reminded Ankush of this. 'I know', he said, 'But you're going to be working with Ani for three days! What are you going to do with him? What plans have you made?' I explained that my plan involved three elements...

1 **Calibration:** to get in tune with the client, find out where they're at and 'get' their world;

2 **Connection:** to find your way into a feeling of connection with them (and vice versa); and

3 **Education:** to allow yourself to be guided by wisdom and insight about how to share the principles behind clarity with them.

Figure 12.1:   The CLARITY® Claibration Model

I told him that my primary goal with a client is to create a space where they can have an increase in their clarity of understanding; a jump in consciousness that will give them what they need in order to solve their problems and create the results that matter to them. I explained, 'In any domain, your embodied understanding of how life *already works* is going to make the difference between freedom and frustration, between struggle and success'. I told him…

Your embodied understanding of the mind is the ultimate leverage point for creating meaningful results, and living a life you love.

Ankush didn't really believe me; he was convinced there had to be more to it than that. The client was an entrepreneur who'd bought a company and managed to double its turnover and profitability in just two years. But Ani's business success had come at a high price. He'd been working 16-hour days, and almost never took a day off. He was feeling stressed, pressured and worried about the future. During the first morning of our coaching intensive, I asked him, 'What's your explanation of what's been causing your feelings?' Ani wrote an exhaustive list of causes on the whiteboard (see table). Once he'd finished, I asked, 'Would you like to hear *my* explanation for your high levels of stress?' I wrote on the whiteboard, '100% of your feelings are an experience of THOUGHT in the moment'…

Misunderstanding/Illusion/ Trick of the mind/La-la Land	The reality you're built for/ Fact of life/Pre-existing truth
My client's explanation of what was causing his feelings of stress, pressure and worry…	My explanation; the actual cause of his feelings of stress, pressure and worry…
 – Business – Money – Banks – Extended family – Lack of time – Staff – Customers – Changes in legislation – Past events	You're living in the experience of the principle of THOUGHT taking form in the moment. 100% of your feelings are an experience of THOUGHT in the moment. 0% of your feelings are coming from anything *other than* THOUGHT in the moment.

- Future issues
- His own personality
- Personal shortcomings
- etc

Ani told me he'd have to reflect on that, so we paused for lunch. When we resumed, he walked up to the whiteboard and put a huge X through his list of 'causes' and said, 'I get it. I've been doing it to myself. I've been feeling my own thinking and *believing* I was feeling my list of circumstances! I don't have a stress problem anymore. What are we going to do with the rest of the three days?'

Ankush's jaw nearly hit the floor…

Misunderstanding complexifies; understanding simplifies

An 1817 issue of the highly esteemed *New England Journal of Medicine* included an article called 'Practical Remarks on Some of the Predisposing Causes, and Prevention, of Puerperal Fever, with Cases'. Puerperal fever (aka 'childbed fever') was a hideous infection afflicting one in four women who gave birth in hospitals during the eighteenth and nineteenth centuries, often resulting in the death of mother and infant. The race was on to identify the causes, and the article listed a wide variety, ranging from constipation and vigorous exercise to long journeys and the weather.

The list of spurious causes was accompanied by a list of spurious preventative measures, including avoiding exercise, avoiding bodily motion, reducing food intake, hastening delivery, inducing vomiting and bloodletting. The one true cause (bacteria) and the appropriate preventative measures (antiseptic procedures) were missing. Why? Because the role of germs in causing illness was not understood. Doctors of the day routinely carried out autopsies then conducted internal examinations on pregnant women without first washing their hands.

Misunderstanding/Illusion/ Trick of the mind/La-la Land	The reality you're built for/ Fact of life/Pre-existing truth

Early nineteenth-century medicine's explanation of the causes of childbed fever...
  – Inclement weather
  – Excessive or violent exercise
  – A long or difficult labour
  – Costiveness (constipation)
  – A long journey
  – The state of mind of the mother
  – A mother's predisposition to puerperal fever
  – Miasmas and atmospheres
	Modern medicine's explanation of the causes of childbed fever...
	
	Bacteria on the hands and instruments of the doctors and nurses

Throughout history, people have created theories, stories and myths to explain things they don't understand. When true causes are not understood, spurious causes and solutions proliferate. The moment we believe our experience is coming from something *other than* THOUGHT in the moment, our heads fill up with bogus causes and potential (equally bogus) solutions. The moment we realize the true source of our experience, our heads clear, and we return to the moment.

> *When true causes are not understood, spurious causes and solutions proliferate.*
> *Misunderstanding complexifies; understanding simplifies.*

The fewer assumptions the better

'Occam's razor' is a tool for problem solving favoured by scientists. It suggests that if you have a number of possible explanations for a phenomenon, it's safest to choose the one involving the fewest assumptions. In every scientific field, the discovery of principles – fundamental laws of nature – is a momentous occurrence that eliminates assumption-rich explanations in favour of simplicity, accuracy and clarity. In Chapter 1, I listed three realizations that have brought our understanding more closely into alignment with the truth of life...

- Isaac Newton's insights into the principle of gravity that transformed our understanding of the material world and laid the groundwork for the Industrial Rrevolution.

- The realizations about 'invisible matter' on doctor's hands that prompted Ignaz Semmelweis' pioneering of antiseptic procedures.

- James Watson's breakthrough discovery of DNA's double-helix structure, leading to numerous modern-day applications including agriculture, pharmaceuticals and forensics.

Each of these realizations paved the way for the acceptance of a genuinely *new paradigm* (in the scientific sense of the word): a principle-based 'platform' that scientists could agree upon and use as the basis for further exploration. A principle meets the following three criteria (with thanks to single-paradigm pioneers, Keith Blevens and Valda Monroe):

1 **Constant:** A principle is always true; it never varies.

2 **Explanatory:** A principle provides a complete accounting for how something works; there are no anomalies.

3 **Predictive:** Given the principle, one can predict outcomes in advance.

It stands to reason that when we don't understand the *principles* behind an aspect of life, we innocently generate *spurious explanations* for it. The evolution of human knowledge has been driven by the *realization* of explanatory principles that dissolved a plethora of competing theories and bogus explanations.

Psychology is currently in its pre-paradigm phase

Thomas Kuhn introduced the term 'paradigm shift' in his controversial book *The Structure of Scientific Revolutions*. Kuhn explained that scientific fields go through five distinct phases, the first of which is the 'pre-paradigm' phase. During this phase, research is taking place, but there is no consensus on any one theory. Instead, there are multiple incomplete theories which conflict with each other. The field of psychology is currently awash with multiple incomplete theories, models and methodologies. There are literally hundreds of schools of 'talk therapy', each identifying its own 'causes' of struggle (e.g. trauma, loss, neglect) and the 'treatments' necessary to restore a person to full health (e.g. psychoanalysis, cognitive behavioural therapy, electro-convulsive therapy). The same goes for the domain of personal development, leadership development and organizational psychology. While research is taking place, there is no consensus on any one theory. This is as we would expect: *every* scientific field has competing theories and models during its pre-paradigm phase. In fact, the reason psychology is not currently considered to be a 'hard science' is precisely *because* it is in its pre-paradigm phase. The principles behind clarity represent a *paradigm* for psychology: constant, explanatory and predictive.

The ultimate leverage point

When I checked in with Ankush at the end of the first day, he had a sudden and profound insight. He said, 'Oh! I know why you didn't have a detailed plan for what you were going to do with the client. You knew that his only problem was a *misunderstanding* about where his experience was coming from. All he needed was a realization about how the mind already works, and he'd have the answers he needed'. I congratulated him on this insight. An increase in your clarity of understanding (aka level of consciousness) is the ultimate leverage point when it comes to creating results. This is the aim of the CLARITY® *Impact Model*: an increase in your embodied understanding of the principles behind clarity that brings you the direction, inspiration and creativity to create the results that matter to you.

What we did with the rest of the three days

During the remainder of our time together, we looked at the sticking points and opportunities in Ani's business from this new perspective. One of his issues had been frustration because he often had to tell his staff the same thing, over and over again. But when viewed through the lens of the CLARITY® *Impact Model*, he realized something essential: his staff had been picking up on his stressed-out state of mind *before* he had the chance to say anything. He recognized that nobody does their best listening (or communicating) when they're feeling tense. He discovered that he'd been *accidentally* creating the conditions that found him frustrated and having to repeat himself. During our session, he discovered the power of connection and reawakened his ability to listen deeply to people.

When he returned to work, Ani had a surprise waiting for him. He said that it was almost as though his staff had changed in his absence. He found that they listened to him, and took his suggestions on board. He started organizing his week differently so he could spend time with his wife and young son (in fact, on the Friday after our intensive, he left work at 5pm for the first time in two years). When I followed up with Ani several years later, he told me, 'A lot of the battles I'd been fighting in my mind about potential consequences and fear of the unknown just fell away. Having a clear mind allows me to acknowledge the reality of a situation while staying focused on our strengths and open to insight. Clarity and peace of mind have a calming effect on my team *and* my customers, so we're achieving more as a result'.

Ankush has also experienced a profound transformation. At the time of the intensive, he was enjoying a successful career working for a Global 500 company, but he was passionate about becoming a coach. He started using his understanding of the principles behind clarity to deliver additional value to his employer, while developing his impact as a transformation professional. As Ankush cultivated his entrepreneurial instincts and learned about the 'business' of transformation, his client base grew. At the end of 2014, he intuitively knew that the time was right, so he handed in his notice. Today, Ankush is a successful *Clarity Coach* and a leader in the coaching community. He has spoken at conferences in the USA and Europe, and works with clients from around the world, helping them achieve extraordinary results.

Practicality Check: How is a jump in consciousness going to help me get results?

When we lose sight of the constant, 100% nature of the thought–feeling connection, our heads fill up with spurious explanations and dubious tactics to resolve them. The moment we wake up to the truth of the principled nature of our experience, the false explanations fall away, and the path forward becomes clear. Your clarity of understanding is the ultimate leverage point for experiencing a clear mind, more of the time, with all the considerable benefits that brings.

So if we're already built for reality, what stops us making progress? If children are born with an intuitive understanding of these principles, why do so many people struggle to create the results that matter to them?

Bottom line results: 'What's the number one result that you perceive would have the biggest positive impact in your business?' While there may well be important operational issues to address, an increase in your clarity of understanding is the *ultimate leverage point* for creating meaningful, sustainable results. Your *embodied understanding* of the inside-out nature of the mind has an 'across the board' impact on your work, and on your life in general. In a world where the outside-in misunderstanding is being reinforced wherever we turn, your understanding of how your mind *really* works will turn out to be one of the most valuable things you've got going for you.

---

keep exploring ❖ connect with others
share your discoveries ❖ deepen your understanding

Experiment: Part 1 – Imagine if we could send a 16 year old from the present day back to 1817. If the doctors and nurses allowed them to,

---

our teenager could have a bigger impact on the health of humanity than the best-educated doctors of the day. Why? Because of our teenager's embodied understanding of the pre-existing fact of germs. At first, it would seem to the medics as though our teenager's suggested actions (scrub up, sterilize your instruments, wear surgical masks, clean that filthy operating theatre, use sterile dressings etc) were random and without reason. Yet those actions would result in a massive reduction in infection and a corresponding increase in health. While the doctors had already been doing their best to get good results at their existing level of understanding, an increase in their embodied understanding of the fact of germs would eliminate misinformation and massively increase the quality of their results.

Part 2 – Let's assume that 200 years from now, psychology will have assumed the status of 'hard science'; that the principles behind it will be as widely and well understood as germ theory is today. Now imagine what would happen if a 16 year old from the 2200s was sent back to the present day. Our future-teen could have a bigger impact on the psychological health of humanity than the best-educated psychologists of the present day. Why? Because of our teenager's embodied understanding of the pre-existing fact of the principles behind our psychology. At first, it would seem to us as though our teenager's suggestions (get a better understanding of these principles) were random and without reason. Yet this would result in a massive reduction in stress and a massive increase in clarity, insight, performance and results. While we'd have already been doing our best to get good results at our existing level of understanding, an increase in our embodied understanding of the fact of psychological principles would eliminate misinformation and massively increase the quality of our results.

Fortunately, we don't have to wait for a time-traveling teen. The principles behind psychology have been discovered, and as you continue realizing them for yourself, the results will be inevitable.

www.jamiesmart.com/results12

13

The Only Two Challenges that Stop People Making Progress

....

Overthinking: the art of creating problems that aren't even there.

Internet meme

'Where do you believe your experience is coming from?'

I was in a hurry. I was due to collect my car from the mechanics at 5:30pm and take my daughters for dinner and a movie, but when I got to the garage, the car wasn't ready. 'It'll be ready in five minutes, mate – we're just running some final checks'. I knew better than to argue, and took a seat in the waiting room, but my head was swirling with urgency and reproach. *Why didn't I arrange to pick the car up earlier? How were we going to get to the movie on time? Why did I try to squeeze so much in today?* I peered into the garage to see my vehicle elevated six feet in the air on a car lift, with two mechanics attending to it with a hammer and a blowtorch. What kind of 'final check' was this? I instantly saw this was no five-minute job. My heart sank even further and my head went into overdrive. *What's wrong with my car? Why am I such a bad father? Why does everything always have to be so difficult? Why do I always do this?* I started pacing around the garage to try and dispel some of the tension and anxiety. Suddenly, a quiet voice spoke from the depths of my being...

'Where do you believe your experience is coming from?'

I stopped in my tracks. *'Did you believe your feelings were letting you know about the car, or the mechanics, or the movie, or your daughters? Did you believe your feelings were letting you know about your past, or your future, or what you're like as a person?'*

In a heartbeat, I fell out of my contaminated thinking and back into the moment. I called my ex-wife and explained I'd be late, and asked her to feed the girls; that I'd be picking them up shortly and taking them to the movie.

The solution to my predicament was obvious once I fell out of contaminated thinking. We're built for reality. Our intelligence and wisdom is always there, ready to guide us the moment we wake up to reality. The only thing that gets in the way is contaminated thinking, arising from the outside-in misunderstanding. We all have areas in our lives where things flow effortlessly, and other areas where we struggle. There's a way in which all my clients have the same two challenges when I first meet them. You're about to realize the only two challenges that ever stop people making progress, and the unexpected key this realization holds for creating results.

Challenge one: Preoccupation

When I first meet a potential client, they're typically preoccupied with something. This preoccupation can take many forms, but one thing's usually clear; they've been thinking about it. A lot! Brooding, ruminating, trying to figure it out. They've given it a lot of thought, and that's usually made matters worse. Here are some examples of the kinds of things people have been thinking far too much about:

- I want to get slim, fit and healthy, but I keep falling back into bad habits.

- I'm desperate to improve my money situation, but nothing seems to change.

- I'm trying to find the right relationship (or fix my current one).

- I'm trying to find my purpose in life, my true calling.

- I need to get more clients.

- I want to raise morale in my company, and get people more engaged.

- I've been thinking about starting my own business.

- I'm trying to change my limiting beliefs.

- I'm trying to figure out what our competitors are planning to do that could knock us out of the game.

- I want to play a bigger game but I don't know what it is.

- I want to spend less time at the office and more time with my family.

- We need to disrupt our industry before someone else does.

- I want to change our company culture but nothing seems to work.

By the time they get to me, they've usually chewed it over, written checklists and ordered multiple books from Amazon about it. Sometimes they've made progress in all kinds of other areas, but *there's this one thing* that they just don't feel they're progressing with (or at least, not in the way they want to).

Challenge two: Underestimation

Similarly, when I first meet my clients, they tend to radically underestimate their talents, abilities and innate capacities. And do you know *where* they tend to overlook their talents and abilities the most? You guessed it – in the area where they're preoccupied. Typically, they have a number of aspects of their life where they do really well. If we go through their personal histories, we find numerous examples of stellar qualities, including...

- Natural leadership (sometimes in 'crunch' situations where many people would crumble).

- Creativity and innovation, finding elegant solutions to problems.

- Wisdom, intuition and gut-feel, bringing them clarity of direction in times of uncertainty.

- Resilience and resourcefulness (often in the face of extremely challenging circumstances).

- High performance (often at tasks that would have others trembling with trepidation).

- Love, connection, kindness and compassion.

- An innate capacity for realization and insight that shows up exactly when they need it.

I've never met a person who *didn't* have examples of these kinds of qualities. It sometimes takes a little time and curiosity to find them, but they're *always* there. Yet when it comes to the area of their lives where they've been perceiving themselves as 'stuck' or 'struggling', people tend to overlook the fact that they're connected to these powerful resources.

The unexpected solution

We've been conditioned to seek additive approaches, so when I explain the two challenges, the next question is usually, 'So how do I fix that?'. But there's a more useful question to ask first:

'Why do people get stuck in these two challenges in the first place?'

The answer to this is simple: contaminated thinking arising from the outside-in misunderstanding. This profoundly deceptive 'trick of the mind' is responsible for challenges one and two, and is the cause of the majority of problems we face as individuals, organizations and societies. The solution is a deeper embodied understanding of the principles behind clarity; an intuitive feel for the inside-out nature of how your mind and perception *already works*.

Implication-based Learning

So how do you deepen your embodied understanding? Let me introduce you to what I call *Implication-Based Learning* (IBL). You've already been doing IBL your whole life, but you may not have had a distinction for it until now. IBL is the learning that takes place *automatically* when you're exposed to sensory data (like a human version of the machine-learning algorithms that are increasingly shaping our digital environment). Obvious examples include how you learned to walk and talk, even though no-one 'taught' you how to do them. Let's look more closely at this:

Gravity
Gravity is a pre-existing fact of life. It doesn't care what you think about it; it's completely impersonal. You were born into gravity, and from the moment you were born, the implications of gravity were 'obvious'; while you couldn't see gravity, you couldn't miss its effects. As a result, an *automatic* IBL curve was initiated. You started learning about the implications of gravity within moments of being born, and you've continued learning about those implications to this day. By the time you were six or seven years old, you had developed

such a deep, *embodied understanding* of the implications of gravity that you were able to use that understanding without even thinking about it. Application became automatic. In fact, you've probably relied on your embodied understanding of gravity to do many hundreds of different things in the past week, without even thinking about it (e.g. picking up a cup, sitting in a chair, walking down a flight of stairs). That's how powerful your grounding in the *fact* of gravity is; a grounding that you developed effortlessly and automatically through IBL and benefit from *without even thinking about it.*

When you learn by implication, application is automatic...

Germs

My friend and colleague, Katherine Breuss, told me a fascinating story about her pre-schooler who was learning about germs. The child's teacher had a brilliant idea; at the beginning of the day, she put glitter on two of the children and said 'Let's see where the glitter is by the end of the day'. Of course, by the end of the day, all the children were *covered* in glitter. The teacher explained that germs spread in the same way, except that germs are invisible. Germs are a pre-existing fact of life. We're born into a world of germs but, *unlike* gravity, germs are non-obvious. For most of history, humanity was painfully unaware of germs. So before an automatic IBL curve can be initiated, germs and bacteria need to be made 'visible' to us. This is what the brilliant teacher did – she made the *invisible* germs *visible* to the children using the metaphor of glitter. And while the method was probably different, this is what happened for you too. Somebody made germs visible to you, and an automatic IBL curve was initiated. Eventually, application became automatic. In fact, you've probably relied on your *embodied understanding* of germs and bacteria to do dozens of things in the past seven days, without even thinking about it (e.g. washing your hands, cleaning a surface, applying the three-second rule). That's how powerful your grounding in the *fact* of germs is; a grounding that you developed using IBL and benefit from daily *without even thinking about it* consciously.

When you learn by implication, application is automatic...

The principles behind clarity

Like gravity, the principles behind clarity are a pre-existing fact of life. You're born into them. But *unlike* gravity, the principles are non-obvious; they're invisible (like germs, only more so – you won't see the principles of MIND, CONSCIOUSNESS and THOUGHT using a microscope, because they're what's *creating* your experience of what you *see* when you use a microscope). The purpose of this book (and of all my work) is to make these principles 'visible' to you so that an automatic IBL curve is initiated, and you start benefiting from a deep embodied understanding of these principles. That way, *application becomes automatic.* As your embodied understanding of the principles behind clarity deepens, you get to benefit from that understanding throughout your day *without even thinking about it.* This is the source of the kind of clarity that leads to meaningful results.

Domain	Pre-existing fact of life?	Obvious?	IBL curve
Gravity	✓	✓	Initiated automatically via implication-based learning
Germs and bacteria	✓	✗	Need to make it 'visible' first, then it progresses automatically via IBL
Inside-out nature of life/the principles behind clarity	✓	✗	Need to make it 'visible' first, then it progresses automatically via IBL

There are aspects of life where you *already* perform brilliantly; where you trust yourself to respond intuitively in the moment. For one person it might be cooking, project management or graphic design. For someone else it might be parenting, driving or public speaking. The difference between the areas where you struggle and the areas where you thrive is simple:

In the areas where you've been struggling until now, there's been a big gap between your embodied understanding and reality.

In the areas where you thrive, there's very little gap between your embodied understanding and reality.

Let's take public speaking as an example. An enormous percentage of the population are afraid of public speaking. If you ask them why, they'll give you a long list of reasons ('What if I don't remember what to say? I'm nervous in case I look stupid. I'm worried about what people are thinking about me'). When they see someone for whom public speaking is effortless, the nervous speaker assumes that the confident speaker is finding *answers* to all those questions and concerns, but that's not the case. Ask a confident speaker what they're thinking about when they're in front of an audience, and they'll usually say 'Nothing'. They're typically in an open, responsive state of mind with their attention on the audience and how their message is landing. Remember: when true causes are not understood, spurious causes and solutions proliferate.

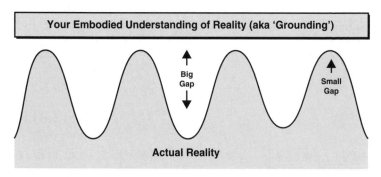

Figure 13.1: Grounding: Your Embodied Understanding of Reality

Your mind is a self-correcting system

We all have places in our life where we have a good embodied understanding of the self-correcting nature of our minds. Have you ever said something like one of the following?

- 'I'll sleep on it and see how the situation looks in the morning'.

- 'I'm not thinking clearly; I'll call them when I'm not feeling so annoyed'.

- 'Don't worry; it'll all look different in a few days'.

- 'I'm not getting anywhere. I'm going to take a break and come back to it with fresh eyes'.

These kinds of statements represent your *intuitive* understanding of the self-correcting nature of the mind. It's just that until now, you may not have realized just how reliably your state of mind can return to clarity. As you continue deepening your understanding of these principles, you're going to benefit from this innate capacity more and more.

So what's this got to do with impact?

Grounding is the foundational piece that allows you to have a profound, transformational impact on another person (whether as a leader, parent, coach or colleague). When you listen to people who are extremely successful in a given field, you'll hear them pointing to an intuitive understanding of these principles (their grounding) without even realizing it…

'You don't learn to walk by following rules. You learn by doing, and by falling over' (Richard Branson)

'You miss 100% of the shots you don't take' (Wayne Gretsky)

'Follow your instincts. That's where true wisdom manifests itself' (Oprah Winfrey)

'Be yourself; everyone else is already taken' (Oscar Wilde)

'And most important, have the courage to follow your heart and intuition' (Steve Jobs)

'There are times when a leader must move out ahead of the flock, go off in a new direction, confident that he is leading his people the right way' (Nelson Mandela)

'You have to do what you dream of doing even while you're afraid' (Arianna Huffington)

'There is only one way to avoid criticism: do nothing, say nothing, and be nothing' (Aristotle)

'We don't see things as they are, we see them as we are' (Anaïs Nin)

Like gravity, the principles behind clarity aren't something you 'do' or 'apply'; they're already there; something you realize for yourself. These principles are already playing out in your work, your relationships, and in every other aspect of life.

You're already swimming in the intelligence and wisdom of life. We're living in these principles like fish are living in water.

Your grounding is what governs the impact you're able to have, and how you're able to leverage it. I often speak to aspiring transformation professionals who are passionate about making a difference to others. They know what they'd love to do, but say they don't know how to make a living from it. What initially looks like a commercial problem (e.g. 'How do I get clients?') usually turns out to be a grounding issue. As your grounding deepens, you find it much easier to resolve the commercial challenges.

Practicality check: How is understanding these two challenges going to help me get results?

In the domains where we're stuck in the outside-in misunderstanding, our minds are preoccupied with spurious causes, and we innocently underestimate our innate capacity for clarity, wisdom and insight. In the domains where our embodied understanding is more closely aligned with the inside-out nature of life, we realize our innate capacities, thrive and create the results that matter to us. Misunderstanding complexifies; understanding simplifies.

CLARITY equals **CAPACITY** minus **CONTAMINATION**

Figure 13.2: The CLARITY® Equation

Your innate capacity for realization deepens your grounding by bringing you more closely into alignment with reality. The more aligned with reality you are, the easier it is to make progress and create results. So once you're making progress, what do you do on those occasions when you get knocked off-track?

Bottom line results: 'Institutionalized overthinking' appears to be an occupational hazard for many organizations. Businesses that are agile and responsive are less preoccupied and more aligned with their innate capacities. It can be liberating to realize that preoccupation is *always* the result of a simple misunderstanding. You have (and everyone in your organization has) the capacity to realize the one way the mind already works, and wake up to the truth of your innate capacity for clarity, insight and high performance.

keep exploring ∻ connect with others
share your discoveries ∻ deepen your understanding

Experiment: Identify some of the areas in your life where you already flourish and thrive; some of the things you find easy. These may even be things that you find so easy that you don't understand why other people are impressed by your abilities. These are areas where you already have an intuitive understanding of the principles we're exploring. Isn't it nice to know that you already have places in your life where you deeply get this?

www.jamiesmart.com/results13

14

Finding Your Bearings When You Get Knocked Off-track

....

DANGER: Keep your fingers out of the machinery.

Health and safety notice

'You're going to have to raise your game...'

It was the end of the first hour of a one-to-one coaching intensive with Jim Lewcock, CEO of The Specialist Works. We were just about to go for a break when Jim dropped his bombshell, 'You're just regurgitating your book; you're going to have to raise your game'. I thanked him for being forthright with me, and said I'd reflect on what he'd said. We were at a serene and luxurious hotel in the Surrey countryside, but as I started walking around the grounds, I felt anything but tranquil. *What was I going to do?* I thought I'd already been bringing my A-game for the past hour, but I didn't seem to be having much impact. I felt worried and anxious. *What if I wasn't up to it? What if I couldn't help my client?* A flashmob of thoughts filled my head with visions of refund cheques, negative word of mouth and a long drive home with my tail between my legs. The feelings of worry and anxiety were getting stronger when I suddenly realized what was going on...

Your feelings aren't telling you about your client, your past,
your future or what you're like as a person...
Your feelings are an experience of the principle of THOUGHT
taking form right now, in this very moment.

As the realization landed, my body started to relax and I began reflecting on the first hour of our session. As I replayed it in my mind, I saw that I'd been struggling to feel a deep connection with Jim. We'd had good rapport when we'd done our intake call earlier in the month, so I started wondering about why it would be different now. Maybe he was feeling under pressure to get maximum value from this investment of his time, money and trust. Jim is a classic entrepreneur – a quick, creative action-taker. Perhaps he was trying to fit what we were talking about into his existing 'mental filing cabinet'. Suddenly, inspiration struck; I knew what to do.

When Jim and I reconvened, I told him I'd realized what the problem was. I said, 'You're here for transformation. You want results, but you're not going to get them by collecting a bunch of new concepts and ideas. The thing that's going to make a difference to you is a *realization*; a deeper insight into the nature of your mind and your life. It's not going to come from me, my stories or my concepts; it's going to come from *inside you*. If you want that, you're going to need to raise *your* game and find a new way of listening. My job is to create a space where I can point you in the direction of that *inner* source of insight and realization. *Your* job is to listen as deeply as you can, and do your best to look in the direction I'm pointing'.

As I spoke the truth I was seeing in the moment, Jim fell out of his urgent, outside-in thinking and back into reality. The feeling of connection we'd had during our intake call re-emerged, and we started to make progress.

Your mind is a self-correcting system

We all lose our bearings from time to time, whether it's dealing with a difficult relationship, handling an unexpected situation or supporting a challenging client. But fortunately, your mind is a self-correcting system. We each have a kind of 'inner sat-nav' that allows us to keep our bearings when the going gets rough, and return to clarity quickly when we *do* temporarily lose our way.

Imagine a river that's being polluted by sewage from the outflow pipe of a factory. Upstream from the factory, the river still flows clear and pure. But downstream, the river is contaminated with toxic waste and the wildlife is suffering. Downstream, you could do your very best to clean the riverbanks and heal the wildlife, but your efforts would have no lasting effect while the factory is still contaminating the water with its noxious sewage. The solution is clear: *shut down the factory!* As it's toxic output starts reducing, the river becomes less and less contaminated, and something wonderful starts to happen; the natural ecosystem starts to *cleanse and heal itself.*

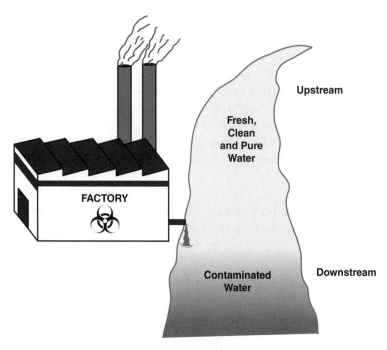

Figure 14.1:   The River of Consciousness

And how is it able to cleanse and heal itself? Because at the river's *source* is a flow of fresh, clean, pure water. Whenever the outflow of contamination is stopped, even for a moment, the source of fresh clean water starts refreshing the ecosystem and clarity emerges. Why? Because clarity is the water's natural state.

Clarity is your mind's natural state.

I don't usually 'unpack' analogies, but this one is worth looking at directly...

- The outside-in misunderstanding is the 'factory' that contaminates the river.

- Contaminated thinking is the 'sewage' the factory produces.

- The river's source is MIND, the intelligent energy behind life.

- The river is the principle of THOUGHT, creating our perceptual experience and connecting us to that source.

- Attempts to clean the river are the *additive*, outside-in methods we use to try and change our felt experience, *after* it's been contaminated (the psychological equivalent of trying to un-bake a cake).

- Shutting down the factory represents the *subtractive* effect of a deeper embodied understanding of the principles behind clarity.

Sydney Banks points repeatedly to the principle of THOUGHT as the creative agent that unites us with the world we perceive, and with the source of all experience, saying 'THOUGHT is the missing link that gives us the power to recognize the illusionary separation between the spiritual world and the world of form'.

> *Your experience flows from and is directly connected to*
> *MIND, the source of fresh, pure perception.*
> *When you fall out of contaminated thinking, even*
> *for a moment…*
> *That source of pure being starts refreshing your awareness,*
> *and clarity emerges.*
> *THOUGHT is the river that unites you with the world you*
> *perceive, and with the source of pure being.*

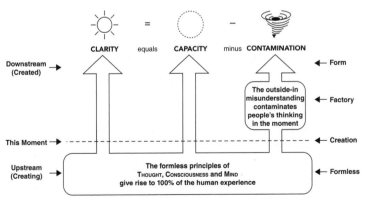

Figure 14.2:   The Mountain of Creation

How to clear your mind

Your mind is a self-correcting system. The only thing that *ever* slows the process of self-correction is the mistaken belief that we're feeling something *other than* THOUGHT in the moment. So what do you need to do to clear your mind? Keep your fingers out of the machinery and continue deepening your understanding of the principles behind clarity. As your insights and realizations continue to update your embodied understanding, you'll find your mind's self-correcting system restoring you to clarity more and more quickly and easily. If you want a universal example of this, look at how quickly and effortlessly small children get caught up in contaminated thinking (tantrums, fears, shyness) then self-correct to clarity, curiosity and contentment. They are benefiting from exactly the same self-correcting system as you and me; they just haven't had the time to build a rigid 'game plan' for how life works (based in large part on the outside-in misunderstanding).

In fact, many of the biggest problems in our lives, our organizations and our world are the result of our misguided *attempts* to find peace, security and clarity using outside-in methods; to try and 'un-bake the cake' of the thinking we've already done…

- The entrepreneur who smokes a cigarette or sucks on a vape to 'relax' and ends up hooked.

- The teenager who uses social media to 'connect' and becomes obsessed with others' validation.

- The manager who uses alcohol to medicate 'work-related stress' and starts making mistakes on the job.

- The sportsperson who cheats because they believe their wellbeing is dependent on winning.

- The CEO who's so focused on 'hitting the number' that they lose their top talent.

- The parent who 'comfort eats' to quash feelings of anxiety and gains excess weight.

- The dictator who wages war on his own people to safeguard his sense of security and success.

A dangerous assignment

The patterns of misunderstanding are a reflection of two 'flavours' of the outside-in misunderstanding.

Flavour 1: It often seems like a person's feelings of stress, boredom or emotional discomfort are coming from somewhere *other than* THOUGHT in the moment (e.g. from their workload, their boss, next week's meeting, last week's argument, their bank balance, their childhood, what they're like as a person).

Flavour 2: It often seems like a person's feelings of relief, peace and excitement are coming from somewhere other than THOUGHT in the moment (e.g. from a drink, a drug, a cigarette, gambling, sex, food, habitual behaviours).

In both instances, it seems like our feelings are coming from somewhere *other than* THOUGHT, but that's not how it works. We're always living in the feeling of THOUGHT in the moment, even when it *appears as if* our feelings are coming from somewhere else.

As soon as we assign our unpleasant feelings to a cause *other than* THOUGHT in the moment, we innocently reinforce the *false belief* that we are separate from and at the mercy of a world 'out there' in space and time, with power over how we feel. It then seems sensible that we look 'out there' for a solution.

We *all* get tricked by the outside-in misunderstanding; we're innocently walking around in a THOUGHT-generated perceptual reality, and relating to it as an *actual* reality. But as you continue waking up from this misunderstanding, you're going to find yourself falling out of contaminated thinking more and more quickly and easily. And when you fall out of a contaminated Narnia, where you land is *reality*. And why is that important?

Because you're built for reality and optimized for results. You've evolved to survive, transform and thrive. When you land in reality, you discover you have what you need to deliver the goods (in fact, it often looks less like 'wisdom' and more like 'common sense'). And this isn't just true for *you*. It's true for everyone on the planet. Your colleagues, clients and customers. The people you lead, manage or coach. Your family, friends and lovers. Everyone.

> *Just as we were born into the principle of gravity, we were born into the principle of* THOUGHT.
> *And just as all seven billion people on the planet are wandering around in gravity...*
> *All seven billion of us are wandering around in* THOUGHT.

So what does this have to do with impact?

Clarity of connection and clarity of thought are universal. We all have times when we experience a deep connection to others, and an effortlessly clear mind. But as you continue deepening your clarity of understanding, you're going to find yourself *effortlessly* spending more time in the moment, with your innate self-correcting system waking you up when you *do* get caught up in your thinking. And what does this have to do with impact?

> *Your impact is a function of your clarity of thought, connection and understanding.*
> *As your level of consciousness continues increasing...*
> *Realization and insight will return you to the present moment...*
> *The domain of clarity, connection and impact.*

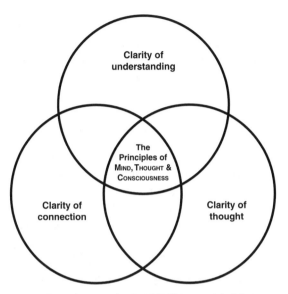

Figure 14.3:   The CLARITY® Impact Model

Reality check

'Hang on a second – if the system is self-correcting, why have I been stressed out for years? My system must be on the blink, because it hasn't been correcting'. Don't underestimate the power of the outside-in misunderstanding to keep people in suffering for days, months and even years. While there are often moments of peace, clarity or levity in the midst of 'depressive periods' or the 'constant stress' reported by many employees, they can be short-lived. Why? Because the outside-in misunderstanding is compelling and being reinforced by marketing, media, friends, family and our own perceptual system. The only thing that *ever* gets in the way of your mind self-correcting is the outside-in misunderstanding.

Just as an embodied understanding of the nature of germs helps create the conditions where your body's self-correcting system can restore you to good physical health...
An embodied understanding of the principles behind clarity helps create the conditions where your mind's self-correcting system can restore you to good psychological health.

Keep your fingers out of the machinery, and keep deepening your understanding of the principles behind clarity. As you do, you'll discover that implementation is automatic, and you'll find yourself benefiting from your mind's self-correcting ability more and more.

Think less, achieve more

A lot has happened in the three years since Jim's coaching intensive. He says, 'Allowing my thoughts to settle rather than urgently pushing them has led to more authentic, permanent and trusted decision making and engagement. The results of which have been rather wonderful'. For instance, Jim decided to purchase one of his competitors (a multi-million pound risk). Their clarity of understanding meant he and his team were able to move quickly, win over the new employees and double the company's profits in one year. When The Specialist Works' 100 staff were moving to new premises, Jim had a sudden realization that led to him inviting his *employees* to design their new workspaces. The result is an office space that's inherently connected to the company culture, deep engagement from the staff who spend so much of their lives there and a six-figure saving on design fees. Jim explains, 'I'm more patient these days. If it's not absolutely right, I don't push it. I wait until it's right and then I act with total conviction'.

The advertising industry always has unsold capacity, so Jim had an insight and created Goodwill Rocks. He persuaded 20 media companies each to donate £50,000 worth of media assets, then invited large charities to join them. Charities are usually very wary of advertisers and salespeople, but by leading with authentic engagement and connection, they can see Jim's heart is in the right place. Twenty large charities got involved right away so The Specialist Works is now doing business with the charitable sector. Goodwill Rocks is accomplishing in *months* what would have taken Jim's team *years* to do using traditional thinking, and has already created a million pounds worth of value for charities. The Specialist Works ended up being selected as one of the *Sunday*

Times 100 Best Small Companies to Work For in 2015. When I asked him about this, Jim said the reason was simple. 'When you're authentically engaged, stuff really works'.

Practicality check: How is my mind's self-correcting system going to help me get results?

As you continue to have realizations and insights into your innate capacities, your ability to create results increases radically...

- The subtractive nature of this understanding means you have less on your mind.

- With less on your mind, you're more available to realization, wisdom and insight, the source of the best ideas.

- You start to feel more connected with others, better able to listen, serve and impact them.

- You also start getting clearer on what really matters to you, unlocking your inner source of authentic power.

- Eventually, you'll start to realize that your mind's self-clearing capacity is *always* going to be there for you, now and in the future, because it's innate and it always has been. You may even find yourself tapping into a deeper well of inspiration, motivation and courage, a powerful mix when it comes to taking action to create the results that matter to you. Remember...

CLARITY   plus   **ACTION**   equals   **RESULTS**

Figure 14.4:   The CLARITY® Results Model

So how do you tune in to the kind of wisdom and common sense that leads to transformational results?

> **Bottom line results:** In Chapter 11, we looked at the link between state of mind and performance. The mind is a self-correcting system, evolved to *automatically* default to clarity. The high-performance states of mind (calm, happy, energized) are natural for you and everyone in your organization. While it's inevitable that you'll get caught up in contaminated thinking from time to time, it's also inevitable that your mind will self-correct to clarity. This is a built-in function of your mind; you can count on it.

> ### *keep exploring ❖ connect with others*
> ### *share your discoveries ❖ deepen your understanding*
>
> **Experiment:** In the 'river' metaphor, we explored the notion that the principle of THOUGHT is an unbroken connection between the world of form that we perceive, and the fresh, pure source that gives rise to our perception. What happens when you reflect on the fact that this is happening <u>right now</u>, in your experience, second by second? That the world of form is being created in your awareness, real time, moment by moment using the power of THOUGHT?
>
> *www.jamiesmart.com/results14*

15

Making Good Decisions: Wisdom, Intuition and Common Sense

··

Follow the wisdom that's inside, because you know as much about truth as any other human being.

Sydney Banks
Author, philosopher, welder

'I don't know...'

My client had come to me because he was stuck, and didn't know how to move forward with his life. He'd been trying to make an important decision for many months, but the more he'd thought about it, the more entrenched he'd become. But now that same sense of stuck-ness had permeated our coaching session. My questions were easy, but my client's answers kept coming back the same way. 'I don't know'. One of the keys to having a transformational impact with an individual or a group of people is getting into a feeling of connection with them. When you've got a clear head and a good feeling, you can allow that connection to emerge by following your curiosity and asking the questions that occur to you. This way of 'tuning in' to how someone sees the world was so normal to me that I was flummoxed. It wasn't working! My clear head and good feeling were rapidly being replaced with stress and irritation. *Why couldn't he just have a guess? He was a bright guy; why was he being so difficult? I was totally committed to helping this person, but couldn't he at least meet me halfway? Why wouldn't he just answer my questions?* We were stuck. He didn't know what to answer, and I didn't know how else to engage him. As my frustration grew, a new thought popped into my mind...

Where do you believe your experience is coming from?

In a flash, I fell out of the La-la Land of my judgmental, contaminated thinking and landed back in reality. 'Your feelings aren't letting you know about a difficult *client*', I realized. 'They're letting you know about *difficult thinking*; the principle of THOUGHT taking a "frustrated" form in the moment'. Feelings of humility and compassion washed over me as my client transformed before my eyes from 'difficult and uncooperative' to 'feeling insecure and doing the best he can'. It was suddenly plain to see that he felt worried and anxious. Why hadn't I been able to *see* that just a few moments earlier?

When you fall out of the illusory non-reality of contaminated thinking...
Where you come to rest is the present moment; the reality you're built for...
A domain rich with wisdom, intuition and common sense.

When it comes to deciding what's right for you and your life, nobody has more access to wisdom than you. Not your parents, not your friends, not your priest, not your partner. Not your government, not your boss, not your teachers, and not me. From Napoleon to Nelson Mandela... from Oprah to Elon Musk... the world's greatest result-creators are guided by wisdom, intuition and gut-feel. As you start tuning in to this 'common sense', you'll realize just how ever present and available it is when you're free from mental clutter. Wisdom also turns out to be one of your most reliable 'advisors' when it comes to having an impact with other people.

When you get out of your own way, the next step is obvious

The moment I woke up to reality, I knew what to do. I explained that there's a flavour of 'I don't know' that's rich and juicy, with a sense of wonder and curiosity. At the other end of the spectrum is a flavour that comes with stress and pressure; like when a teacher asks you a question in front of the class that you're *supposed* to know the answer to, but don't. He nodded and said his were more like the second kind. I said, 'I'm sorry, I should have explained. Asking questions is just my way to get a better sense of how you see life. I want to get on the same page with you, and for us to find a relaxed feeling of *connection* with each other. There are no right or wrong answers'. He visibly relaxed, and we started chatting. The sense of connection emerged and we started making progress. As each of us fell out of our contaminated thinking, we relaxed into wisdom. I was guided in how to work with my client, and as he fell out of contaminated thinking, he suddenly got clarity on the way forward for him.

How to make good decisions

As the world becomes more complex, volatile and uncertain, the consequences of our decisions become increasingly ambiguous, and we all have times when we find them challenging to make. Some decisions seems trivial (e.g. choosing your breakfast, a pair of socks or what movie to watch). Some seem more significant (e.g. selecting a holiday, buying a car or accepting a promotion). Some can seem enormous (e.g. moving in together, changing careers or starting a new venture) and some have consequences that are truly vast (e.g. cutting jobs, exiting the European Union or going to war). But here's the thing: while different decisions bring different consequences and levels of complexity, there's nothing in *reality* that makes one decision more difficult than another...

The outside-in misunderstanding is the main source of difficulty in decision-making...
But as you fall out of the complexity of contaminated thinking...
You fall into the simplicity of wisdom and common sense.

People aren't good at predicting emotional responses

Research reveals that people do poorly when it comes to predicting their emotional states in future scenarios. We fall prey to a variety of cognitive biases, amplifying our expected emotional response to *certain* things while underplaying or even *ignoring* others. While we can passionately believe that we would feel terrible if X happened or wonderful if Y happened, the truth is more fundamental: remember, you can't be a victim of circumstance, and neither can anyone else. We're always going to be living in the experience of THOUGHT in the moment, no matter what.

DISTINCTION: Good luck vs bad luck

There's an old Taoist story about a farmer whose prize mare runs away. 'What bad luck', the farmer's neighbours commiserate, but he replies, 'Maybe, maybe not'. The next day, the horse returns with a powerful stallion following behind. 'What a fortunate man you are', the neighbours say as the farmer and his son corral the two horses, but he is again philosophical. 'Maybe, maybe not'. Later that day, the farmer's son falls and breaks his leg while attempting to tame the wild stallion. 'That really *is* rotten luck', the neighbours tut, but (to their annoyance) the farmer

---

> replies, 'Maybe, maybe not'. A few days later, a general and his troops come to the village and conscript all the young men to fight at the front. All except the farmer's son, who stays at home because of his broken leg. 'You have to admit, that was incredibly lucky', the bewildered neighbours say, shaking their heads at the farmer's mysterious powers as he replies predictably...
>
> *'Maybe, maybe not...'*

While 100% of your feelings are generated from within, the optical illusion of the mind can make it *seem* like they come from the outside; from somewhere *other than* THOUGHT in the moment. While the neighbours perceived the farmer's life as a wild pendulum of good fortune and bad, the farmer remained composed and philosophical. It can absolutely seem like your security and wellbeing is coming from circumstances (e.g. money, jobs, romantic partners), the future (e.g. hopes, fears, uncertainties), the past (e.g. victories, defeats, indiscretions) and even yourself (e.g. physique, health, personality). But all of those factors are *neutral*. 100% of your feelings are generated from within; you're living in the experience of the principle of THOUGHT taking form in the moment.

Reality check

So am I saying it doesn't matter what you decide? No, I'm not. The choices you make can have an enormous effect on your life and the lives of others, today and 20 years from today. Your ability to make good decisions is infinitely improved when you're *not* being hamstrung by contamination from outside-in misunderstanding. When you're hanging out in reality, you *intuitively* realize what you've got going for you.

Freedom from fear of public speaking

I was working with a client who was scheduled to give a talk to a large audience, and was suffering with anticipatory anxiety. The person genuinely believed their feelings were giving them feedback about the future event. This, despite the fact that the future event didn't exist in *reality*; it only existed as a plan in the present. While there was certainly a high degree of probability that the event would happen, the talk would not exist in any real or factual way until several weeks later, when the client walked onto the stage. There was no place in the client's present *reality* where the talk existed; it only existed as an idea. While they could certainly *believe* they were feeling the future event, they were actually feeling THOUGHT in the moment.

> *The issue isn't that we sometimes have uncomfortable*
> *feelings arising from* THOUGHT *in the moment…*
> *The issue is that we sometimes believe there's more to it*
> *than that…*
> *That our feelings are arising from something <u>other than</u>*
> THOUGHT *in the moment.*

Think about it: if you tell someone you're in a particular state of mind (e.g. happy, sad, excited, angry, grateful, stressed, love), they typically ask a variant of 'Why?' or 'What about?'. We've been innocently conditioned to look to the outside for a reason. Whether the 'outside' we point to is our circumstances, the past or the future. Whether it's our physical body, our personality or our habits. We've been trained to look away from the true source of power that's *creating* our experience, and assign the cause somewhere else. We feel a feeling and assume, 'There's no smoke without fire; there must be *something* out there that's causing this'. But the world of form is neutral; it's totally incapable of creating a feeling. Your experience is the creation of THOUGHT in the moment, brought to life by CONSCIOUSNESS. When it comes to our feelings, there *is* smoke without fire. The smoke of our feelings is giving us moment-to-moment feedback about the ebb and flow of THOUGHT, *not* about the 'fire' of circumstances, past, present or future. And it raises an important question…

> *What quality of decision making can you expect when a*
> *person is basing their decisions on misinformation?*

When people mistakenly believe in a La-La Land, many of their predictions and decisions are fundamentally flawed, contaminated by misinformation. For example...

- When people mistakenly believed in a *flat earth (La-la Land)*...

- When astronomers mistakenly believed in a *geocentric universe (La-la Land)*...

- When chemists mistakenly believed combustion was caused by *phlogiston (La-la Land)*...

- When doctors *mistakenly believed* infection was caused by *miasmas (La-la Land)*, with disastrous consequences for their patients' physical health...

Similarly, when you and I *mistakenly believe* in an *outside-in world* (La-la Land), many of our predictions and decisions are fundamentally flawed, contaminated by misinformation.

Back to reality

But here's the thing: the moment we fall out of contaminated thinking and back into the present, the quality of the information we're basing our decisions on increases exponentially. How often have you...

- Been unable to remember someone's name, no matter how hard you try, then suddenly recall it after you stop thinking about it?

- Been struggling with a problem and finally given up on it, only to realize what the solution is a short time later?

- Grappled with a decision that went around and around in your head, then had an insight about the way forward while you were doing something else entirely?

Reality check

'Wait a minute...' I hear you say. 'What about when someone gives me the creeps, or I suddenly get the sense that I shouldn't go down a particular street. Are you really saying that's just THOUGHT?' Yes and no. We have our senses for a reason; they give us essential information about reality that we calibrate to so we can survive and thrive. If you see a fire engine speeding towards you, step out of its way. 100% of your *experience* of the fire engine is THOUGHT-generated, but there are massive physical-world implications if you get hit by one. And consider this: who's more likely to accidentally step in front of a speeding fire engine: someone who's present and aware, with a clear head and in touch with reality? Or someone who's preoccupied with contaminated thinking? When you're present and aware, THOUGHT is free to do what it does best: guide you through reality in this game we call life.

Should I really just follow my wisdom?

Sometimes I meet people who have asked someone for advice and been told 'just follow your wisdom'. But what if it was wisdom that had them ask for advice in the first place? There are many domains in life that require specialist training, technical information and know-how. Just as you wouldn't want an untrained doctor to perform brain surgery on you by 'following their wisdom', there are many areas where we can benefit from other people's knowledge and expertise. Wisdom doesn't eliminate the need for knowledge or expertise, but it can be an excellent guide in selecting how and when to *acquire* that knowledge and expertise. Wisdom and common sense are a phenomenal guide when used by someone who has also developed a high level of skill. Here's an example: a while back, I decided I wanted to develop more muscular strength. I'd done some weight-training over the years, but usually ended up injuring myself after a short period of time. I didn't want to repeat that pattern, and I had a realization. 'You haven't established sustainable habits because you didn't have an embodied understanding until now. Once you develop an embodied understanding, it will sustain and support you for the rest of your life'. As I saw the truth of this, I knew exactly what to do. 'Hire a great trainer!' I found someone highly skilled who could teach me exactly what I needed to know and help me get the embodied understanding I needed to develop in a sustainably healthy way.

Practicality check: How are wisdom, intuition and common sense going to help me get results?

We're constantly immersed in the principle of THOUGHT, just as we're constantly immersed in the principle of gravity. It stands to reason that the decisions we perceive as most important are often the ones where we get tricked by the outside-in illusion. But that raises a beautiful possibility: the answer you need is closer than you think. While some decisions can involve more complex scenarios than others, misunderstanding adds an *exponential* level of complexity to any decision. Conversely, *understanding simplifies*, subtracting contaminated thinking, and waking you up to the wisdom and common sense you were born with. As clarity emerges, the quality of your decisions increases. And the decisions you make can have a massive impact on the actions you take and the results you're able to create.

CLARITY plus **ACTION** equals **RESULTS**

Figure 15.1:   The CLARITY® Results Model

So now that you're navigating by wisdom, you're all set to take your results to a whole new level.

Bottom line results: the ability to make effective decisions is crucial in business. The quality of the information a decision is *based* on will have an impact on the quality of the decision. It can be both humbling and enlightening to realize that a percentage of the decisions we've made in our lives have been based on *misinformation*; 'noise in the system' arising from the outside-in misunderstanding. The more truth there is/less misinformation there is in your decision-making process, the more effective your decisions will be. While misunderstanding adds complexity to decision making, understanding simplifies. It subtracts complexity and reconnects you with reality, wisdom and common sense.

keep exploring ⁙ connect with others
share your discoveries ⁙ deepen your understanding

Experiment: What are some of the times when you suddenly realized the answer to something that you had struggled with until that point? Did the realization come with a sense of truth or 'knowing'? People will often report that they 'just knew' it was the right solution, and that it came to them out of the blue. It can be empowering to discover that your capacity for insight and realization is innate. As your understanding continues to deepen, you're going to find yourself coming to rely on it more and more.

www.jamiesmart.com/results15

16

The Source of Impact, Innovation and Disruption

Today, if you're not disrupting yourself, someone else is; your fate is to be either the disrupter or the disrupted. There is no middle ground.

Salim Ismail
Author, entrepreneur and angel investor

' "Uber protest" by black cab drivers brings traffic chaos to Westminster...'

London's black cab drivers are renowned for being the finest in the world, in large part due to their having to learn 'The Knowledge' – an extraordinary feat involving the memorization of over 25,000 streets, 300 routes and numerous points of interest. The Knowledge originated in 1865, takes an average of 34 months to learn and must be passed before the driver can be licensed. The *Guardian* headline from 26 May 2015 reported black cab drivers' protest against Uber, the app that's rapidly disrupting the taxi trade in over 300 cities around the world. But from the moment the first consumer satellite navigation systems started coming on the market in the 1990s, the writing was on the wall for The Knowledge.

Airbnb.com was valued at $25 billion in November 2015, making it more valuable than Hyatt Hotels or the InterContinental Hotels Group (owner of Holiday Inn and Crowne Plaza). This despite the fact that Airbnb has a fraction of the number of employees and owns no hotels. It's safe to assume that Hyatt and Intercontinental had been keeping tabs on each other for years in order to identify competitive opportunities and threats. But the potential for an Airbnb was in the wind from the early 2000s, as Web 2.0 started giving rise to the virtual communities, social networking sites and user-generated content of the 'sharing economy'.

The music industry's revenues dropped by 50% between 2001 and 2010. The executives held tight to their outdated business model, like sailors in a hurricane clinging to the mast of their sinking ship. In the end, Apple came to the rescue and the creation of the iTunes Store helped establish it as one of the world's most profitable companies. But as far back as 1999, Napster and other file-sharing services were foreshadowing the storm that would decimate the music business.

Of course, it's easy to appear wise with hindsight. We incorrectly assume that, because the data was available, these turns of events were predictable and to be expected. But that's not the case. One of the reasons there are so few Ubers, iTunes and Airbnbs is because of how very *difficult* it is to accurately predict the future. Strategy can be a powerful and important tool for creating a successful venture. But where does great strategy come from? Data is part of the equation. But the hospitality industry, the taxi industry and the music business all had access to the data. Great strategy comes when you add the other piece of the equation: exponential insight. As you get a deeper understanding of exponential insight, you unlock its power to create competitive advantage and exponential results.

The strategy equation

I was scheduled to deliver the keynote speech to kick off a strategy workshop for the council of the Institute and Faculty of Actuaries (IFoA). The IFoA has over 25,000 members, and its council had been charged with developing strategy for the future of the profession. Actuaries are renowned for being extremely detail-oriented, data-driven and analytical; they also love playing devil's advocate. The chief executive wanted me to inspire some fresh thinking, new perspectives and innovative ideas. I reflected to myself...

- How can you meet these people where they are?

- How can you make it easy for them to look in the direction you're pointing?

- How can you make it a no-brainer for them to come on the journey?

When I arrived at the venue, the council members were chatting casually over coffee, so I introduced myself to several small groups and started asking them questions: questions about their profession, themselves and the challenges they faced. Questions about their hopes for the strategy workshop, and for their future. I listened as deeply as I could to each person, and I started feeling connected to them.

Early in the talk, I set the context, saying 'I understand you've been given the job of setting the strategy for your profession. This means that if you do a good job, your colleagues 20 years from today will be blessing you, and if the profession goes off a cliff, they'll be cursing you. Is that correct?' They nodded, and I started telling them about Airbnb, Hyatt and the exponential impact of digital technology. I told them about Allstate Insurance, which had put up a $10,000 prize for the first team who could beat its insurance algorithm (an algorithm developed over 60 years by some of the world's finest actuaries and data scientists). More than 100 teams competed for the prize, and after *three months* Allstate's algorithm had been optimized by over 270%, saving the company tens of millions of dollars in annual costs. Allstate had the data, but that was only half the formula.

Now I had their attention. I asked them if they'd like to know the formula for strategy, and they nodded eagerly. I wrote…

Strategy = Data + Insight

They assured me that they were already great at gathering and analysing data, but that they weren't so familiar with the second part of the formula. So I asked them, 'When do you get your best ideas?' I've asked thousands of people this question, ranging from parents to therapists, from athletes to leadership teams. The answers are always the same…

– In the shower	– Working out at the gym	– When the plane leaves the runway
– In the bath	– Running or riding	– Connecting with other people
– Dropping off to sleep	– Relaxing with friends	– When I stop thinking about a problem
– Waking up in the morning	– Sitting by the ocean	– When I'm doing something else
– Travelling to and from work	– On holiday	– etc
– Walking in the woods		

We're *built* for exponential insight! But it doesn't come from the shower, the holiday or the walk in the woods. It's a natural capacity that we all have. You've been having insights and realizations your whole life, but when we attribute them to external factors (walks, woods, workouts) we limit our understanding of just how available insight is. As you reflect on some of the realizations that have already made a big difference to you in your life, you'll start to realize just what a powerful source of intelligence you have going for you. And that's good because...

We are now living in a VUCA world

As digital technology continues developing at an exponential rate, our world is changing accordingly. The acronym VUCA was coined by the US Army War College to describe the kinds of scenarios the military have been finding themselves in since the 1990s. The term has been adopted more recently by businesses and futurists because we *all* now live in a VUCA world: a domain of *volatility*, *uncertainty*, *complexity* and *ambiguity*.

Alfred Korzybski (creator of general semantics) served as an intelligence officer during the First World War. He realized that while the *technology* of war was progressing at an astonishing rate, the social structures, organizations and habits of thinking that gave *rise* to the war were not progressing. In the 100 years since Korzybski's insight, technology has progressed at a dizzying rate. Today we have computers, drones, smartphones, nanotechnology, hydrogen bombs, artificial intelligence, life support machines, virtual reality and more. Our technology is accelerating exponentially, but our societal understanding of thinking and perception is still stuck in the Middle Ages.

> At our *current level of consciousness, entrusting
> humanity with exponential technology is like giving
> a toddler a loaded machine gun.*
> We need a new understanding of how our minds work to
> navigate the challenges of volatility, uncertainty, complexity
> and ambiguity.

DISTINCTION: Linear thinking vs exponential insight

If you were to place one grain of rice on the first square of a chessboard, two on the second, four on the third and so on, doubling every time, something surprising would happen. By the time you get to the 64th square, you would need hundreds of *billions* of grains of rice. This surprises us, because we've been conditioned to think in terms of linear increments rather than exponential jumps. But digital technology has no such limitation. Computing power grows exponentially: it doubles in speed and halves in size and cost roughly every 18 months (a function known as Moore's Law). Our *intellects* have evolved for the linear world we've lived in for most of human history. But digital technology is driving us at high speed into a VUCA world that requires a new, more leveraged way of thinking.

While **linear thinking** can be useful, it has an inherent limitation: its only reference point is the past; the thoughts you've *already* had. All too often, we approach strategy, goal setting and problem solving by identifying problems and solutions from our *current* level of consciousness, then setting out to solve them from the same perspective. By definition, linear thinking is blind to the present moment, and the implications of what's happening *right now*. We're riding the wave of the information revolution; a wave powered by *exponential* technology. When Airbnb launched in August 2008, the team didn't have access to better *data* than Hyatt. They didn't have a bigger budget or more experience. What they *did* have was **exponential insight**: realizations that aligned them with reality and allowed them to discover the future of accommodation.

Stephen Hawking, Elon Musk and Bill Gates have all expressed concern about the enormous risks to humanity that artificial intelligence poses. We have to recognize and harness the power of **exponential insight** if we want to sense and respond to the challenges of the digital age. We have to understand the *nature* of THOUGHT if we are to survive and thrive as individuals, as organizations, as societies and as a *species*.

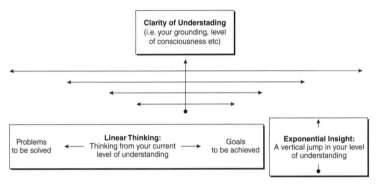

Figure 16.1:   Exponential Insights Enable Exponential Results

In his excellent book *Strategic Intuition*, William Duggan (a senior lecturer in business at Columbia Business School) attributes the dubious popularity of the 'audacious goals, unwavering self-belief and massive action' school of thought (as discussed at the start of Chapter 7) to a rags-to-riches myth in American culture. This myth started in the 1800s and has been recycled by 'success gurus' ever since (despite the fact that it's often a surprisingly unhelpful attitude when it comes to accomplishing something big). He suggests that a much more rational approach is to prepare for opportunity, see it when it shows up and act on it. Duggan explains that when you prepare for opportunity, you open yourself to the arrival of flashes of realization; the exponential insights that are found over and over again at the source of some of the biggest achievements in history. From Archimedes' bathtub 'Eureka!' to Newton's apple-tree insight... from Napoleon's victory at the Battle of Austerlitz to Bill Gates' insight into the future of computing. As you continue exploring the inside-out nature of reality, you'll find yourself waking up to a healthier and more impactful understanding of who you really are and the life you're living. You're also going to find yourself opening to the same source of exponential insight used by many of the great results-creators throughout history.

Practicality check: How is exponential insight going to help me get results?

You live in a world of opportunity. It appears that most success in human endeavours comes from insight, experimentation and acting on opportunity when it arises. Of course, in order to act on an opportunity, you need to be aware of and prepared for it. As your understanding of the principles behind clarity continues to evolve, you're going to spend more time in the present moment. As a result, you'll be better able to sense how reality is unfolding and more available to exponential insight. Remember: you're built for reality and your mind works one way: inside-out. You won't find wisdom and common sense in the La-La Land of contaminated thinking. But the moment you fall out of contaminated thinking, where you come to rest is reality, the domain of clarity, common sense and exponential insight.

So as your interpersonal transformation continues, it's time to ignite your *commercial* transformation.

Bottom line results: We're used to linear thinking, but we need exponential insight to deal with the challenges of a VUCA world (a world of volatility, uncertainty, complexity and ambiguity). Exponential insights aren't just 'good ideas'; they're fresh new thinking that brings you and your organization more closely into alignment with reality. As such, they are a source of massive leverage. They can cut through the cruft of outdated habitual thinking and align you with the reality of the present moment. When you fall out of contaminated thinking, and come to rest in the domain of exponential insight, there's often a feeling of gentle certainty that lets you know you're on the right track.

keep exploring ⁘ connect with others
share your discoveries ⁘ deepen your understanding

Experiment: When do you get your best ideas? What happens when you open to the possibility that you're always connected to the source of exponential insight?

www.jamiesmart.com/results16

PART THREE

LEVERAGE
Your Commercial
Transformation

You never change things by fighting the existing reality. To change something, build a new model that makes the existing model obsolete.

R. Buckminster Fuller
Designer and inventor

Hope lies in dreams, in imagination, and in the courage of those who dare to make dreams into reality.

Jonas Salk
Virologist, inventor of the polio vaccine

17

Ignite Your Entrepreneurial Instincts

Most people are walking around, umbilical cord in hand, looking for a new place to plug it in.

Cavett Robert
Founder of the National
Speakers Association

'You are the leader of your life, and you always have been...'

The insight hit me like a ton of bricks. I'd been working as a programme manager, leading multi-million pound business transformation projects for five years. It was a good job but I felt stuck. Some of my friends had left their jobs to go self-employed or start their own businesses, but I was convinced that 'doing my own thing' wasn't possible for me. I didn't question why; it just seemed true.

Everything changed one weekend in 1998 when I attended a workshop to improve my influence skills. The trainer stood at the front of the room, relaxed and at ease, sharing engaging stories and insightful perspectives. Watching this skilled 'transformation professional', my first thought was, 'I want to be able to do that'. I became completely absorbed in the learning experience, and at some point in the weekend, I had a profound and liberating insight:

You are the leader of your life, and you always have been.
You can choose the results you want to create.
And live into the choices you make.

I found a six-month contracting role that would give me the extra time and money I wanted to pursue my new-found dream of becoming a facilitator, speaker and coach, then I handed in my notice. I took every opportunity to develop my future skill set and practise it in my day job. I coached my colleagues, ran in-house project management workshops and offered to facilitate challenging meetings for the company directors. One month, I offered to deliver a presentation that needed to be given to 20 different audiences around the organization (despite being terrified of public speaking). By the time I got to the twentieth presentation, I'd lost my fear. I took every opportunity I could find to step out of my comfort zone, create value for the organization and grow. It turns out that paid employment can be a great 'sandbox' where you get rewarded for creating value while you learn and practise *today* the skills you're going to need *tomorrow*.

After two years of this intensive 'incubation' process, I stopped contracting and started my first business. And that's when I discovered *why* I'd spent all that time believing I couldn't do my own thing; that my case was different. Here's why…

The education system is preparing students for jobs that won't exist in 10 years

The education system was originally developed to deliver a numerate, literate and compliant workforce to the factories and offices of industry. Like cogs in a machine, students weren't required to think for themselves; they were required to do as they were told. You can clearly see the ghosts of the factory in the traditional education system's 'production line' approach, with rote learning, standardization and rows of desks. The world of learning gets divided into narrower and narrower subject areas, with no apparent connection to a coherent whole. We're conditioned to believe that:

- There's a 'right way' to do things.
- There's an authority who knows what the correct answers are.
- We should *defer* to authority rather than take the lead.
- We should recite the correct answer rather than develop our own perspective.

This is fine when you're preparing students for a world of work that is well understood and relatively stable. But it's disastrous when you're preparing them for a world that's volatile, uncertain and ambiguous. Whether you work in a large organization or are founding a fast-moving startup; whether you're a student or a sergeant… If you want to thrive in the VUCA world, you need to ignite your entrepreneurial instincts.

So what are your entrepreneurial instincts?

When you hear the word 'entrepreneur', you may conjure up images of high-profile players such as Elon Musk (Tesla), Arianna Huffington (Huffington Post), Richard Branson (Virgin), Oprah Winfrey (Oprah) or Jeff Bezos (Amazon). And while these people are exceptional examples of entrepreneurial talent, we all have access to the same source of 'entrepreneurial instinct' that they do. So what *are* your entrepreneurial instincts? They're expressions of the deep drivers we started exploring in Chapters 1 and 6 (direction, resilience, creativity, authenticity, intuition, presence, connection and clarity). Take a moment to think about some of the qualities we commonly associate with entrepreneurs.

Entrepreneurs...			
Take responsibility	Are intuitive	Have insights	Create results
Take action	Are agile	Have presence	Think big
Take decisions	Are always learning	Have common sense	Think different
Take calculated risks	Are bold and courageous	Create communities	Think for themselves
Take opportunities	Have a purpose	Create experiments	Think creatively
Are influential	Have fun	Create clients	Solve problems
		Create cash flow	etc

A few moments of reflection will reveal that many of these qualities are *natural* for you when you're not caught up in contaminated thinking; inevitable results of grasping the implications of the inside-out nature of life.

Implications drive instincts

As you have realizations into the 100% inside-out nature of how the mind *already works*, you reignite the entrepreneurial instincts that have been with you your whole life...

IMPLICATION 1: You can't be a victim of circumstance

As you realize it's impossible for you to be a victim of circumstance, you become less likely to look to the outside world for security, approval and validation. Fear of failure and fear of criticism are revealed to be all bark and no bite. It becomes easier to take calculated risks, free from confusion about where your wellbeing comes from. You become more carefree, enjoying yourself and having fun as you experiment and explore. As you take action, you take responsibility for creating the results you want to create.

IMPLICATION 2: You're wired for realization; you're an insight machine

As you come to rely on your innate capacity for realization, you start trusting that you're going to have the insights you need when you need them. This innate capacity for realization is the source of innovative solutions to problems. It allows you to see 'the elusive obvious', both at the micro-scale, and at the macro-scale of massive vision and purpose. Reality is changing fast, so it can be a huge relief to discover that you're built to have fresh new perceptions that bring you more closely into alignment with that reality as it evolves.

IMPLICATION 3: We each live in a separate reality

As you start to see that we each live in our own, THOUGHT-generated perceptual reality, the whole domain of 'other people' becomes simplified. You'll start finding it easier to see things from others' perspective – to connect with them and 'get' their world – while staying true to yourself. Being able to understand what other people are up against is an entrepreneurial 'superpower' that allows you to identify opportunities, influence others, create solutions and get clients.

IMPLICATION 4: You're always connected to everyone and everything

As you realize you're always connected to your true self, to other people and to the whole of life, you discover you're an inherent part of this creative, evolutionary intelligence. The only thing that ever obscures this fact is contaminated thinking arising from the outside-in misunderstanding. Your dreams, desires and aspirations exist for a reason; you're part of life and you always have been. As you relax into the truth of this, you become more available to wisdom, realization and common sense. Feeling connected to who you really are, to other people and to life itself starts becoming the norm.

IMPLICATION 5: Your mind is a self-correcting system

As you continue realizing your mind's self-correcting nature, you'll find yourself falling out of contaminated thinking and waking up to reality, more and more quickly and easily. As you come to rely on this powerful capacity, you'll spend less time in unnecessary hesitation, worry and conflict. The result of this unburdening is greater agility and awareness. Decision-making becomes easier as you are freed from the misinformation of the outside-in misunderstanding.

IMPLICATION 6: You're built for reality and optimized for results

You're a born learner, with an extraordinary ability to sense, choose and take action. In fact, the vast majority of actions you take each day (e.g. walking, reading, talking) you do without even thinking about it, because of the depth of your embodied understanding. As your understanding of the principles behind clarity increases, you become more present and aware, with less on your mind. As a result you're going to find yourself sensing, choosing and acting more fully in alignment with what truly matters to you. This is the path to the kind of experiences and results truly worth having.

IMPLICATION 7: Your conception of the future is not reality; now is reality

While it can be wonderful to envision the future, it doesn't actually exist. Our ideas of the future are not reality; they never include the totality of our innate capacities, and of who we really are. As a result, we often overlook a simple fact:

You're built for the reality of the present moment...

When the future arrives, it will be the present moment...

The reality you're built for... the here and now.

People often ask me 'Why aren't we born knowing this?' But we are. The average four year old is far more 'psychologically healthy' than their parents or teenage siblings, intuitively embodying many of the qualities listed above. The *issue* is that we're conditioned into believing in a non-reality; the illusory La-la Land of the outside-in misunderstanding. This is why little children are more 'entrepreneurial' than most adults, and it's great news. Why?

As you deepen your understanding of the principles behind clarity, you reignite your entrepreneurial instincts.

So does this mean everyone can be a high-profile entrepreneur?

At the level of principle, yes, but in practice, there's a more important question... What would you love to have happen? What are you inspired to create? Often, I hear people repeating mantras like this...

- 'I'd do the things that really matter to me, but I haven't got the time.'

- 'I hate my job but I can't get work doing anything else.'

- 'I'd follow my heart if I was guaranteed it would work out OK.'

- 'I'd do what I love but I can't get paid for it.'

- 'I'd be happy if I could find work that fulfils me.'

- 'I'd do something meaningful if I knew how to do it.'

- 'I'd do what I love if only I knew what it was.'

The outside-in misunderstanding wafts through these statements like a bad smell, but as people start waking up from contaminated thinking, amazing things start to happen. You may...

- Discover that you *enjoy* the job you were previously desperate to leave.

- Find yourself working towards an inspiring result, just for the hell of it.

- Take on responsibilities that you'd previously tried to avoid.

- Change direction to do something that wasn't previously on your radar.

- Take action and do things that you wouldn't even have *considered* previously.

Entrepreneurs take responsibility

We opened this chapter with a pithy quote from Cavett Robert, 'Most people are walking around, umbilical cord in hand, looking for a new place to plug it in.' Twenty years ago, I would probably have told you the key was to plug that umbilical cord into *yourself*; to take 100% responsibility for yourself and your results. This is what many entrepreneurs do, and it's one of the reasons so many of them get stressed out, burned out and find themselves back where they started within a couple of years.

While it's important to take responsibility, I now see it differently. Your 'umbilical cord' is *already* plugged into life itself. You're always connected to life and you always have been. If you're willing to take responsibility for (a) prioritizing your own evolution, (b) clearing up the misunderstandings that have been holding you back until now, and (c) moving forward boldly… then life will support you. Just as it has done every step of the way.

Practicality check: How is re-igniting my entrepreneurial instincts going to help me get results?

While we are often comforted by the familiar, we learn from what's new and different. Whether you're working in an existing structure or creating something brand new: your entrepreneurial instincts are what support you in doing something you've never done before; in creating something that has never existed until now. Remember, you can learn things by taking action that you're unlikely to figure out in the privacy of your own head. Your entrepreneurial instincts cut through the theory, and allow you to get impartial feedback from the real world.

Our world is changing more quickly than ever before.
When it comes to creating results,
realization and real-world feedback
are the most reliable information sources that exist.

So once you've reignited your entrepreneurial instincts, who are you going to make a difference to?

Bottom line results: Big companies are often told they should 'act like startups', but this is impractical advice. It makes far more sense for companies to cultivate *the freedom of thought* that startups benefit from by awakening the *entrepreneurial instincts* that are latent in the company's people. The commitment to purpose, willingness to experiment and focus on the customer experience that typify the 'startup mindset' emerge naturally when you ignite your entrepreneurial instincts.

keep exploring ∻ connect with others
share your discoveries ∻ deepen your understanding

Experiment: Reflect on the entrepreneurial qualities we've explored in this chapter. Which ones do you particularly admire or appreciate? Which ones don't you like? Which qualities would you add, alter or remove from the list? Which qualities would you love to have for yourself? Whatever those qualities are, I invite you to open to the possibility that you already have them, in essence. It may be some time since you've used them, but they're still there, waiting to be reignited. And how do you reignite them? Do something. Get started. When you take action from clarity, the way forward becomes clearer.

CLARITY   plus   **ACTION**   equals   **RESULTS**

Figure 17.1:   The CLARITY® Results Model

www.jamiesmart.com/results17

18

Tribal Marketing: Engaging Your Audience

....

*'The goal is not to do business with everybody who needs what you have.
The goal is to do business with people who believe what you believe.'*

Simon Sinek
Author, speaker

'Katherine's got clarity...'

In the six months before my book *CLARITY* launched in February 2013, I would occasionally feel insecure about my lack of a 'social media strategy'. I had many thousands of people in my network of Facebook friends, twitter followers and newsletter subscribers, but I didn't really 'get' social media. One day, a friend of mine made the offhand comment that Facebook was 'all about photos'. As I reflected on her statement, I realized that there was some truth to it; photos did seem to attract more attention than plain text.

As the book launch approached, I started to mobilize my tribe. WHSmith (the UK's biggest book retailer) had selected *CLARITY* as its 'Deal of the Week', so the book was going to be getting pride of place in railway stations, airports and motorway services up and down the country. On 21 February, Amazon started delivering *CLARITY* into people's letterboxes. I was having coffee with Katherine, a colleague whose copy of the book had just arrived in the post, when my friend's words about Facebook and photos came back to me. I took a picture of her holding the book, then posted it with the simple message 'Katherine's got clarity ;-)'

By the end of the day, a few other people had posted photos of themselves with the book and the 'got clarity' message. Within a few days, dozens of people had done the same. As the weeks passed, the Facebook photos became funnier and more creative, with people competing to post the most fun and interesting 'clarity photos'. The sense of fun and engagement continued to grow as people's dogs, cats and tropical fish started to make appearances in the pictures. To my delight, this unanticipated viral outbreak continued to grow and, by the date of the WHSmith launch, there were countless clarity photos circulating on Facebook.

And that's when something very interesting happened. A friend who had been on holiday for several weeks – completely unplugged from the internet – arrived at London's Heathrow Airport to see enormous 'Deal of the Week' posters announcing the book. When he logged on to Facebook, his timeline was filled with pictures of people he knew, proudly displaying copies of *CLARITY*. He was shocked, and sent me a bewildered congratulatory message, saying, 'This is amazing. Your book is everywhere! How did you do it?'

But he was wrong. While the book had sold well, it *wasn't* everywhere; it was everywhere in *his neighbourhood*. The members of his tribe had *CLARITY*, so when he stood in the middle of that tribe, it seemed as though *everyone* had it.

The search for meaning, purpose and belonging

In the past, people looked to certain institutions (e.g. church, government, school, industry, postal service, monolithic companies) and structures (e.g. university education, marriage, job for life) to 'give them' a sense of security, purpose and belonging. But as technological and sociological changes continue to sweep the globe, many of those institutions and structures are either falling into decline, or failing to engage the communities they once served. As we are propelled into the VUCA world, people are searching for that sense of security, purpose and belonging. And they're finding it in tribes: communities of like-minded people who share a worldview.

People are increasingly seeking out individuals, companies, charities and communities who *genuinely* share their values and worldviews. As a result, purpose, authenticity and transparency are becoming more important than ever, and here's the thing: you can't *fake* authenticity. In a time of 24x7 social media and smartphones, people are going to see the real you whether you want them to or not, and this presents a huge opportunity. You see…

> *When you're being who you really are, you shine a beacon*
> *for those who align with you and your worldview.*
> *Your purpose, authenticity and transparency send an honest*
> *signal that resonates with others.*

The spread of the internet and social media has meant that we *all* now have the power that used to be reserved for politicians, for the news media and for captains of industry. A teenager with a smartphone can now command an audience that only used to be available to the most popular TV shows. Leading management thinker Peter Drucker famously said that a business has two core functions that create results: marketing and innovation. If marketing is a way of multiplying your ability to sell something, you can think of *tribal* marketing as a way of connecting with, engaging and giving value to the people you want to serve; a tribe who resonate with your worldview. When you have a highly engaged tribe, it becomes much more straightforward for them to 'buy' what you're offering. This is the case whether you're a student looking to promote club nights at your university or a CEO who wants to engage your colleagues and other stakeholders... whether you're a coach who's keen to build a community of potential colleagues and clients, or a marketing director seeking to create raving fans for your company's products and services.

Tribal leadership

Who are a group of people you want to serve? Entrepreneur, author and marketing philosopher Seth Godin explains that 'a tribe is a group of people connected to one another, connected to a leader, and connected to an idea'. Becoming the leader of a tribe puts you in an extremely influential position. Members of the tribe will give you their attention, their loyalty, their time and their money on an ongoing basis *if* (and only if) you continue to show them that you are worthy of it. And how do you show them you're worthy of it? By *being* worthy of it. This means...

- 'Getting' their reality, understanding their worldview and genuinely caring about the people in your tribe.

- Helping them solve their problems, achieve their goals and get the results that matter to them.

- Being honest, authentic, transparent and trustworthy.

- Being courageous, true to yourself and doing what makes sense to you.

You show you're worthy of being the leader by <u>leading</u>...
By going first and giving value to the people you're
here to serve.

So what audience or group of people would you love to make a difference to? One of the groups I love working with is transformation professionals (e.g. coaches, therapists, trainers, consultants, bodyworkers, nutritionists etc) but I also work with artists, entrepreneurs, company CEOs, sportspeople and members of the public (to name just a few). When I ask transformation professionals about the next group of people they want to serve, they often get anxious and say they're struggling to find their 'niche'. But this isn't about your niche; it's not even about *you*! It's about selecting a group of people you want to *serve*.

Every audience is another room in your mansion

Here's a way of thinking about it: imagine that you've inherited a large and beautiful mansion, with a trust fund dedicated to paying all the running costs. There's only one catch: if you want the trust fund to pay the bills, you have to restore the mansion. There are groundskeepers on staff to take care of the exteriors and gardens, but the rooms are your domain. The rooms are in a shocking state, with torn wallpaper and broken chairs. They need cleaning, painting and decorating. They need furnishing, carpeting and plenty of tender loving care to return them to their former glory. So which room do you want to start with? The lounge or the master bedroom? The kitchen or the billiard room? Once that one's been taken care of, you can decide which one you want to do next. You don't have to *limit* yourself to one; you don't have to stay in it forever. You don't need to make the room part of your identity. You just need to decide which one you want to start with. Then, once you're done, you can decide which one you want to do next.

It's the same with audiences. You don't need to limit yourself to one, or stay with the same audience forever. You don't need to make the group part of your identity. But it can be very useful to choose which one you want to start with; a group you'd love to serve. Then, if you decide you want to increase your domain, you can decide which group you want to serve *next*. Every audience is another room in your mansion.

Remember, everyone is walking around in a separate reality; a THOUGHT-generated *perceptual* reality that they experience as an *actual* reality. People gravitate towards others who have perceptual realities similar to their own. A tribe is a group of people whose values and worldview are similar enough that they find it easy to connect with and relate to *each other*.

What's your story?

Tribal leaders tell *authentic* stories that resonate with the worldview and values of the people in their tribes. These stories turn *off* as many people as they turn *on*; they make it easy for someone to decide whether this tribe is for them or not. For instance…

- In her TED talk, *The Art of Asking*, Amanda Palmer tells the story of her rise from street performer to rock star, and the importance of vulnerability, connection and the willingness to ask for help. Her story attracted plenty of criticism, but the people who resonated with her worldview knew instantly that she was someone they wanted to listen to. Many thousands of her tribe members engage with each other on dedicated Facebook groups *they've* created for the purpose.

- On her *Luxy Hair* YouTube channel, Mimi Ikonn shares fashion and beauty tips, with a focus on hair (*Luxy Hair* is a company that sells hair extensions). The vast majority of Mimi's 2.5 million followers are teenage girls, where her most popular hair and fashion videos can get between 10 and 15 million views. Mimi's videos won't appeal to everybody – most people aren't interested in the best ways to wear hair extensions – but that doesn't matter. Members of her tribe post thousands of comments on the videos, and share the photos Mimi posts to Instagram. At the start of the videos, Mimi greets her tribe, 'Hello my beautiful friends', before giving her hair and beauty tips, *as well as* her values and worldview (on subjects ranging from attitude and diet to lifestyle).

- On their *I Love Marketing* podcast, Dean Jackson and Joe Polish provide a free weekly episode teaching mindsets, strategies and tactics. The early episodes are like a soup-to-nuts sales and marketing masterclass, starting with Joe and Dean's personal stories. Their style isn't everyone's cup of tea, but they have a large and loyal following of entrepreneurs and marketing professionals who listen to their episodes (some of the episodes get hundreds of thousands of downloads). Members of their tribe have even created *I Love Marketing* Meetup groups in cities around the world so they can connect with others who share their worldview.

Your authentic stories also do something else. They make it easier for people to connect with you and relate to you, establishing your credibility to lead the tribe. Why? Because the story you tell resonates with a story your tribe members are telling themselves (or *want* to tell themselves). A story can...

- Meet people at *their* reality, letting them know they're not alone and that you understand their world.

- Establish your credentials, and show why you're qualified to take the lead.

- Explain why they are where they are, and give them reason to be hopeful.

- Illustrate your worldview, and demonstrate your values in action.

- Let them know what's possible, and how to move forward.

Practicality check: How is learning about tribal engagement going to help me get results?

While we can achieve some results entirely under our own steam, many of our most inspiring results involve other people. The bigger the impact you want to have, the more likely you are to need the support of others, whether as colleagues, mentors, sponsors, employees, clients, suppliers, patrons, cheerleaders or community members. Experience shows that people who resonate with your worldview, values and purpose are *far* more likely to support your efforts.

So once you know who you want to lead, how do you make a difference to them?

Bottom line results: Whether you're the CEO of a Fortune 500 company, or a transformation professional working with a select group of clients, there are certain audiences that it's critical for you to connect with. Each person lives in a separate reality: a THOUGHT-generated perceptual reality that they experience as an actual reality. 'Getting' your audience's perceptual reality puts you in a powerful position to connect with and lead them. The more you're able to create value for your audience in a way that's honest, authentic and transparent, the happier they'll be to give you their attention, their trust, their loyalty, their money and their time.

---

keep exploring ⋅⋅⋅ connect with others
share your discoveries ⋅⋅⋅ deepen your understanding

Experiment: It's time for you to identify an audience. Who are a group of people you/your organization would love to serve? Hint: they may be a group of people you're already well acquainted with; people whose values and worldview you share and understand. Remember: it's not about you; it's about choosing the next 'room in your mansion' to work on.

www.jamiesmart.com/results18

19

The Only Things Anyone Ever Pays For

One man's meat is another man's poison.

Ancient proverb

'A True Fan is defined as someone who will purchase anything and everything you produce...'

In his now-legendary 2008 blog-post '1000 True Fans', author Kevin Kelly (founding executive editor of *Wired* magazine) made the case that creators (e.g. musicians, photographers, designers, authors) could make a decent living with a community of just 1000 True Fans. He defined a True Fan as 'someone who will purchase anything and everything' you produce, and explained that if these fans each spent $100 per year, it would generate a $100,000 income. Many in the creative community embraced this message, and used the internet's unprecedented potential for connectivity to build large, devoted followings. And while his message spoke to the challenges faced by artists, there are valuable lessons in it for us all. By the time Kelly's article was published, I'd already spent five years building a tribe of 80,000 people who read my articles, watched my videos and hired me to work with them. As Kelly predicted, a smaller percentage of these were True Fans, purchasing virtually everything I produced. And it turns out that I was not unique. All over the world, people are creating value and getting rewarded for it. There's a universal 'value formula' that's used by everyone, whether they realize it or not. It's used by companies who want to address new audiences and by church

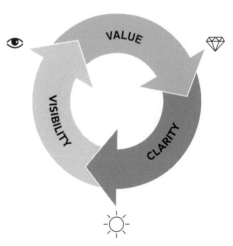

Figure 19.1:   The CLARITY® Value Formula

leaders who want to grow their congregations. Teachers use it to engage their students and teenagers use it to enlarge their social circles. It's employed by terrorist groups to attract recruits and by governments looking to change their citizens' behaviour. The CLARITY® Value Formula has three elements: visibility, value and clarity.

1. Clarity

Clarity of understanding allows you to see through contaminated thinking and move boldly forward to make a difference. Each of us is unique, with our own talents, abilities and perspectives on life. Your uniqueness is an expression of your inner self; the 'true self' we referred to in Chapter 4. This is the source of your authenticity, resilience and common sense. The more aligned you are with your true self, the more impactfully you can create value for others. The only thing that ever stops someone being aligned with their true self is contaminated thinking. But as your grounding in the principles behind clarity continues increasing, you'll find yourself acting from that place of security and certainty more frequently and reliably.

2. Visibility

Value is exchanged in the context of relationships. It's difficult for people to find your products or services if they don't know you or your company exist. It's difficult to create value for people if you don't know *they* exist. If you want to create value for people, you need to become *visible enough* to each other for a relationship to be initiated. You don't need to be visible to *everyone*, but you need to become visible to the people you want to serve. This may mean giving some thought to *who* you want to serve, and *how* you can become visible to each other.

3. Value

People don't pay for what *you* value; they pay for what *they* value. Whether they're paying with money, attention, time or energy; the more highly they value a result, the more they're willing to pay. So what's the value you want to create, and how does it deliver the result your audience is looking for? Understanding how your audience sees reality (i.e. their world view) allows you to create the value that meets their specific wants and needs; the things, experiences and results that matter to *them*.

Case Study: From time-based to results-based

John Wilkes was employed full-time working on marketing, pitch-development and client care for a consultancy. He told me about his dreams of working for himself, with the income and freedom to be truly independent. (John loves the outdoors and wanted to spend less time working and more time fishing.) I started asking questions about John's boss (the owner of the company). 'What results does your boss want?' He told me. 'Why does he want that result? Why does it matter to him?' John didn't know for sure, but took a guess. I asked many more questions, 'What problems keep him awake at night? What issues does he wish would just go away? What are *his* dreams? What does he wish would happen?' John knew some of the answers, but had no idea about others. John realized that, while he'd been working there for many months, he didn't know that much about what really mattered to his employer. I tasked him with finding out and, by the next week, John had made himself more *visible* to his boss and got clarity about what his boss *valued*.

John was working long days for the consultancy (five days a week and sometimes six). As he reflected, he realized much of that time was spent doing things that didn't directly contribute to the results that mattered most to the company. I asked him, 'What could you achieve if you organized your time and energy at work to focus only on achieving the results your boss values?' By our next meeting, John had come up with a plan. If he eliminated all the superfluous activities, and focused only on results, he could deliver what his boss wanted at a much higher level than he was currently doing. Best of all, he reckoned he could deliver these results working only three days per week (though they would still be long days). This would free up two days per week for John to work on his own business and go fishing.

Now came the challenging bit: John didn't just want to move from full-time to three days per week; he wanted to *keep* his existing salary! John was anxious about even *proposing* this to his boss. He worried that it might damage their relationship, or even get him fired. So we worked on his *grounding*. I asked him where he believed his feelings were coming from: the future, his boss's reaction, the thought of getting sacked etc. As we explored the nature of THOUGHT, he fell out of his contaminated thinking and had an insight: he had a strong relationship with his boss, and realized that he would appreciate John being honest and transparent with him. While he still felt a little nervous on the day, he presented his proposal from a place of clarity, authenticity and connection. After taking a few days to think about it, his boss accepted it, later revealing that he'd learned something valuable in the process. John's example underlined that what mattered to his business was *results*. His boss realized that if he could rely on them being achieved to a high standard, then it made sense to pay people for their *results* rather than their hours.

That was six years ago. John now runs a successful digital marketing agency, and has just launched *Hotfishin.co.uk*, a website that connects fishermen with fisheries (imagine a kind of 'Airbnb for fishing'). The fishermen get to explore new runs and book tickets online, while the fisheries get to maximize utilization. He's taken his use of the CLARITY® Value Formula to a new level, becoming *visible* to fisherman and fisheries, and creating *value* for both audiences. His increasing grounding over the years has given him the courage, creativity and insight he needed to take action and play a bigger game. In the process, he's moved from selling his time to selling the results his audience values.

CLARITY   plus   **ACTION**   equals   **RESULTS**

Figure 19.2: The CLARITY® Results Model

Separate realities revisited

Remember: we each live in our own THOUGHT-generated perceptual reality. As you get clarity about who you want to become visible to, it can be profoundly useful to find out more about how *they* see the world. This can help you get clarity about three important things:

1 What they perceive as value.

2 How you can provide that value, or something they'll value even more highly.

3 How you can connect with, engage and educate them to the point where they're able to make an informed decision about what you're offering.

The better you understand your audience's world view, the more easily you can connect with them, and the more eloquently you can communicate with and educate them. Here are some questions that may help you start to 'get' their world view:

- Who do you want to connect with?

- Where do they spend their time?

- What's the result they want?

- Why do they want that result? Why does it matter to them?

- When do they want that result?

- What are their struggles and challenges?

- What are their hopes, dreams and aspirations?

- What are they passionate about?

- What are they afraid of?

- What's important to them? What matters?

- What do they believe? What looks true to them?

- What are they already on the lookout for?

- What's the conversation they're already having with themselves?

- How can you meet them in their reality, and become visible to them?

- How can you inspire them to make themselves visible to you?

Case Study: From searching to finding

At the beginning of 2013, Marina Pearson decided she wasn't going on any more courses. She'd been searching for years and had invested large amounts of time, energy and money, but she wasn't getting a return on that investment. Marina is an author, a speaker and a coach, but she wasn't experiencing the lifestyle, income and sense of fulfilment she'd expected. Then Marina read my book CLARITY and something clicked. She connected with me, joined one of my programmes, and her world started to transform. In the next six months, she...

- delivered a TED talk.

- moved to Bali (one of her dream locations).

- became pregnant after trying for years with no luck.

- started running workshops and filling them easily.

- started signing up longer term coaching clients for the first time, and enjoying the process.

Let's look at Marina's journey through the lens of the CLARITY® Value Formula:

- *Clarity:* while she had plenty of skills and information, Marina was caught up in the outside-in misunderstanding. She had contaminated thinking in some common areas, including money, sales, visibility and 'being enough'. As you start waking up to where your experience comes from, you start to see more clearly who you really are, and what you're capable of. This is what started happening for Marina.

- *Visibility:* as a result, she became more aware of the opportunities that were *already* there for the taking. We're surrounded by opportunities, but when we're caught up in contaminated thinking, we often overlook the possibilities that are right under our noses (or shrink from them when we *do* spot them). Marina started noticing opportunities, and saying 'yes' to them. While this sometimes brought up feelings of insecurity, her grounding meant that she saw through them more easily, or moved forward in spite of them. She stopped taking her contaminated thinking as seriously as she had previously. And this resulted in...

- *Value:* Marina was able to share her unique gifts and abilities with the people who resonated with her. Because she was visible to them (and vice versa), they were able to experience the value she created for them. This led to some of those people wanting to have *more* of what she offered, so she started saying 'yes' to bigger opportunities, and taking on bigger challenges.

After years spent searching and struggling to make a living, Marina found the inner source of fulfilment and security, and had her best year yet (both experientially and financially). She said, 'Best of all, it's happened effortlessly, without me even noticing. Without the kind of stress and effort I'd always thought it would take. I've finally been able to stop searching and start living the life of my dreams!'

Of course, when you take on bigger opportunities and challenges, it sometimes shines a light on areas where you're *not* seeing the inside-out nature of life, and it's time for another increase in your grounding. *The CLARITY® Value Formula* is a virtuous circle. As you grow in any one of the three areas, you're inspired to grow in the others.

Practicality check: How is *the CLARITY® Value Formula* going to help me get results?

If the results *you* want are in any way reliant on other people, *the CLARITY® Value Formula* will help you engage them in your efforts.

Whether you're selling your ideas to your boss, your services to your clients or your values to your children, this formula can help you get clarity, engagement and results.

So once you know what journey you want to take people on, how do you influence people to come on the journey with you?

Bottom line results: Leading management thinker Peter Drucker famously commented that 'because the purpose of business is to create a customer, the business enterprise has two – and only two – basic functions: marketing and innovation. Marketing and innovation produce results'. *The CLARITY® Value Formula* has three elements: Visibility (marketing), Value (innovation) and Clarity (being the person or organization who can deliver the value to the audience). As such, *the CLARITY® Value Formula* is a universal formula for business results.

keep exploring ⁑ connect with others
share your discoveries ⁑ deepen your understanding

Experiment: Over the next few days, you might like to start looking for examples of *the CLARITY® Value Formula* in action. Where are people or organizations deliberately making themselves visible to you? To others? Where are people or companies inviting you to make yourself visible to them? What kinds of value are they offering? What kind of increases in their grounding/clarity of understanding are supporting them in becoming visible and creating value in this way? What are some of your ideas about how you can start becoming visible to your audience? What are some of the ways you can already start to imagine creating value for them?

www.jamiesmart.com/results19

20

Influence, Motivation and Zero-Pressure Persuasion

People are silently begging to be led.

Jay Abraham
Consultant, author

'Put up your hand if you don't like selling...'

Whenever I ask this question, the majority of the audience raise their hands. Even when I'm working with the members of a *sales* team, it's surprising how many of them have an aversion to this crucial element of professional life. When I investigate, I inevitably discover that their experience of selling (or being sold to) involves some form of creepiness, manipulation or pressure. In a nutshell, they feel bad about it. So bad, in fact, that it gets obscured with euphemisms for selling and for the people who do it (e.g. client engagement specialist, business development manager, account growth executive). And yet, whatever you call it, the process of selling is not only essential to enrolling other people in your initiatives but, done effectively, it's also one of the most powerful ways there is for you to serve others. Whether you're selling your services to your clients, or your ideas to your colleagues... Whether you want to persuade an entire market to buy your product or your teenager to make a wise choice about their education... the ability to influence others is an essential skill for results-creators.

It's not about you

So why do people so often feel uncomfortable with the idea of sales, persuasion and influence? Because most of our models of persuasion and influence are of it being done *badly*. The word 'selling' conjures up images of cheap-suited double-glazing hucksters using high-pressure manipulation tactics. We recoil at the thought of having to trick, bully or cajole people into doing what we want them to do. But that's not what effective influence even *looks* like. Our societal image of what it means to be influential is based on faulty, out-of-date models.

Influence isn't about getting what you want by pressuring, cajoling or bullying...
It's about helping people get what <u>they</u> want through connection, education and collaboration.

You see, people don't want what matters to *you*; they want what matters to *them*.

> *People don't pay for what you offer...*
> *They pay for the transformations they desire...*
> *The stories that reflect their values...*
> *The results they want to create...*
> *And the way they want to feel.*

The payment can take many forms, including (but not limited to): money, attention, time, labour, expertise, barter, connections, endorsements, introductions, referrals and prestige. What people pay for can also take a variety of forms...

- While a dealer may be selling a car, the purchaser may be paying for safety (Volvo), speed (Bugatti), school-run status (Range Rover) or prestige (Lamborghini), as well as the feelings and narratives that accompany those experiences.

- While a supermarket may be sourcing organic vegetables, the shopper may be paying for their future health, a delicious meal, a feeling of vibrancy or the opportunity to tell themselves an authentic story (e.g. about caring for their own health, the health of their children, the ethical treatment of animals or how they deserve something a little bit special).

- While a software vendor may be selling a new package, the CTO he's selling to may be buying a feeling of security, the sense that they've made a good decision or that they haven't made a bad decision (when I worked in the IT industry, people used to half-joke that 'nobody ever got fired for buying IBM').

- While a shoe manufacturer may be producing luxury footwear, their customers may be investing in their self-image; a story they're telling themselves about confidence or coquettishness, about seduction or style. They pay for the results they want to experience through buying the shoes, as well as the opportunity to tell themselves that story and experience the feelings that come with *that*.

And this is the key: the only things anyone ever pays for are the transformations they desire, the results they want to create, the stories they want to tell themselves and the way they want to feel.

The secrets of ethically effective influence

In Chapter 9, you read about Pete Bryceland, the coach who struggled with selling. He explained that, when he was having a conversation with a potential client, things would go smoothly. He'd listen deeply to the person and would feel really connected with them. He'd pick up on where their sticking points were and help expand their perspectives so they could see new possibilities. Pete would often identify something that he felt pretty sure the client would value highly enough to invest in coaching with him. It would all be going beautifully. Then, when it came time to talk about money, and about the person becoming a client, it would all go horribly wrong. Pete would start feeling uncomfortable and uneasy. Then the *client* started feeling uncomfortable and uneasy.

Unsurprisingly, when conversations went this way, they rarely resulted in Pete signing up a client, and he felt frustrated. When I talked it through with him, I told him he had good reason to be hopeful. I said, 'You already have everything you need to become a master of ethical influence; you've just had something getting in the way'. And what gets in the way? Contaminated thinking. When it comes to persuasion, influence and selling, your personal history will reveal a universal fact: your experience of the *influencer* is a major factor in whether or not you go ahead with a purchase. If you're like the majority of people:

You don't like being influenced by a person who...

- you feel uncomfortable with or pressured by.

- you don't like, don't trust and don't feel connected to.

- is a poor listener.

- doesn't care about you or the relationship, and only has their own interests at heart.

- doesn't know what they're talking about.

- is unwilling or unable to take the lead, and wants you to do it for them.

- is committed to you doing what's *right for them.*

You like being influenced by a person who. . .

- you enjoy interacting with.

- you like, trust and feel connected to.

- is a good listener.

- cares about you, the relationship, and has your best interests at heart.

- knows what they're talking about.

- is willing to gently lead you in a direction you want to go.

- is committed to helping you arrive at the decision that's *right for you.*

The number one influence factor

Everybody knows that one of the biggest factors when it comes to buying something is the experience the client has of being influenced by you. If they have a great experience of you influencing them, they're much more likely to buy what you're selling.

So what's the biggest factor that determines whether or not a client will have a great experience of being influenced by you?

The experience *you're* having of influencing them. People pick up on 'where you're coming from'. If you're feeling needy, uncomfortable and manipulative, they'll feel creeped out, uncomfortable and manipulated. If you're feeling calm, connected and inspired, they'll feel calm, connected and inspired.

Are you a good listener?

Most people overestimate how good they are at listening. We've all been told that we've got two ears and one mouth, and to use them in that proportion. But the fact is that most people aren't listening; they're waiting for their turn to speak. One of the things I've found with a lot of people is that when they're having a sales conversation, they're up in their head worrying about how much to charge, whether the person can afford it, what to offer, whether they're going to be rejected, whether they're going to hit their sales target etc. This kills connection. One of the keys to impactful influence is putting your attention on the client, by listening to them. When you truly listen to another person, you fall out of your insecure, self-centred thinking and fall into a feeling of connection with the person you're listening to. Connection carries its own credibility; as the feeling of connection emerges, your client's trust in you deepens, and they'll tell you more about what really matters to them. Listening and connection are the key to 'getting your client's world', and to discovering what's valuable and important to them.

Activate your influence accelerant

People tend to buy from those they know, like and trust. The experience of connection is like an 'influence accelerant' that communicates warmth, credibility and trustworthiness. Why? Because true connection is incredibly difficult to fake. While people can easily mimic the 'symptoms' of rapport (e.g. matching and mirroring body language), the felt experience of genuine connection is far more difficult to simulate. As a result, the sense of connection is an 'honest signal' that telegraphs authenticity, credibility and trustworthiness.

Clarity of connection gets you online

The less you have on your mind, the greater your experience of connection is likely to be: connection to the other person/people, connection to your true self and connection to *life* itself. When you're feeling connected, you're 'getting online' to the principle of MIND; the wisdom and intelligence of life. Think about it: no matter how good your phone, laptop or tablet is, its power and value is amplified *exponentially* the moment you go online. As soon as you go online, you step beyond the limits of the information that's *already* been loaded to your device, and open up to an infinite source of *new* information. It's the same with us. The moment we fall out of the La-la Land of the thinking we've *already* done, where we land is an ocean of fresh, up-to-the-minute intelligence. Whether you call this wisdom, common sense, realization or insight, it's one of the most leveraged sources of influence there is. When you're feeling connected to an individual or group, you're much more likely to hit on exactly the right question to ask/the right thing to say. As a result, you have a much better chance of uncovering what really matters to this person, and having the realizations and insights that will serve you both in the course of the conversation.

The secret of zero-pressure persuasion

The feeling of connection is like a 'conduit' for powerful communication. It helps create a space where people can fall out of the La-la Land of their fears and anxieties, and fall into alignment with what really matters to them. This is the domain of education and collaboration. I love having zero-pressure sales conversations, so I'll sometimes ask a prospective client to help me out, saying, 'I want us to have a zero-pressure conversation, so I need to ask you a favour: if you feel even an *ounce* of sales pressure while we're talking, will you let me know?' In any conversation, hidden anxieties and insecurities are the things most likely to diminish connection. When you let people know it's OK to speak their insecurities (or go further, and enlist their support in keeping the connection strong), it's like throwing the curtains open and letting sunlight stream into a dark room. Nobody likes to feel pressured, wheedled or manipulated. Everybody likes to feel seen, respected and treated fairly.

When it comes to communication, persuasion
and influence...
The feeling of connection is like the coal-miner's canary...
It lets you know when you're safe to proceed...
And when it's time to come up for air.

Case Study: Recovering a client relationship

Juan Jose Quesada works as an account executive for a large multi-national that makes enterprise software. He experienced a profound transformation after participating in a weekend workshop with me, and booked a place on my coach training programme the following week. A week after that, he emailed my office saying he'd decided not to proceed with the programme. I was puzzled at his change of heart, so we scheduled a Skype call.

When Juan first appeared on-screen, his arms were crossed and he seemed abrupt and defensive. This was in stark contrast to the warm, connected experience we'd had last time we'd spoken. 'What do you want from me?' he asked. 'Why are we having this call?' Unbeknownst to me, Juan had googled me and read that I was a 'master of influence'. He was afraid that he might be manipulated during our call, and had even written a note to himself warning him not to re-enrol on the programme. His anxiety and tension were obvious; he was caught up in contaminated thinking.

I explained that I'd enjoyed connecting with Juan, and that while I liked the idea of him coming on the programme, what I most *cared* about was our relationship. I assured Juan his money would be refunded within the next 24 hours, and said that the training programme was off the table for now; that I wouldn't even be attempting to re-enroll him during this call. He began to relax, and the sense of connection started to re-emerge. We talked about the insights he'd had, his hopes and dreams and about what he planned to do next. By the end of our conversation, the earlier discomfort had evaporated and we were feeling the deep sense of connection we'd enjoyed previously. The relationship was intact.

A week later, Juan reached out to say he'd had *another* change of heart. He'd been deeply impacted by our conversation and impressed by my commitment to the relationship. He said he definitely wanted to go ahead with the programme. Since then, Juan has trained as a *Clarity Coach*, and is now working with entrepreneurs and company directors in the Spanish market.

Professionals can deliver the goods

People often ask me what it takes to sign clients up for 'high-ticket' products, programmes and services. I reply that it's very simple: you need to let your client know that you can 'deliver the goods'; that you are/your organization is a credible, competent and appropriate collaborator for them to work with. The person will often say, 'We're really good at what we do. We can deliver the goods. How do I let the client know that?' I tell them that's very simple too. 'Once *you* truly know you can deliver the goods, your *client* will know you can deliver the goods'. When someone hires you, they're paying for the results they want to experience in their lives. You need to have the *inner certainty* that you can either (a) support them in creating what they want to create or (b) support them in creating something that will *eclipse* what they wanted to create. Your clients will pick up on that certainty (or lack of it) and act accordingly when it comes to the sales process.

Ask for what you want

A key element of sales, persuasion and influence is the call to action. Whether it's asking for the order or inviting someone on a date, you need to give people the opportunity to take the next step. I'm mentioning this obvious point because, while it may *sound* like common sense, it's astonishing how often contaminated thinking (masquerading as fear of rejection) obscures it.

A key point: every aspect of what you do with your client is part of the client experience: your marketing, your sales process, your delivery, your referral process, your follow up. All of it. The more pristine your client's experience is when they're with you, the more smoothly everything goes in your client relationships.

Practicality check: How is influence, motivation and zero-pressure persuasion going to help me get results?

The ability to influence is one of the keys to creating results that involve others. But many people struggle to be influential in the very places where it's most important. If your result involves other people, you need to be an influencer.

So once you've influenced someone to come on the journey with you, and you have an idea about how you can deliver their dream result, how do you turn your idea into a reality?

Bottom line results: Persuasion and influence are essential business skills. Whether you're looking to influence shareholders or suppliers, colleagues or clients, the most influential people can have the greatest impact. The art of influence starts with finding out what matters to the other person. People don't want what *you* want; they want what *they* want. The transformations they desire, the stories that reflect their values, the results they want to create, and the way they want to feel. Start there.

keep exploring ❖ connect with others
share your discoveries ❖ deepen your understanding

Experiment: What are the people in your audience already on the lookout for? What are the problems they're *already* seeking solutions to? The results they're *already* looking to achieve? If you can determine what your audience perceives as valuable, important and desirable, it becomes much easier to present what you offer in a way that is attractive, relevant and compelling to them.

www.jamiesmart.com/results20

21

Turning Ideas into Reality

....

The future cannot be predicted, but futures can be invented.

Dennis Gabor
Physicist, engineer, winner of the Nobel
Prize in Physics, 1971

'The goal is to eradicate chronic psychological suffering globally for everyone by 2030...'

I felt overwhelmed by the churn of emotions: worry, excitement, anxiety, inspiration. My first book had sold tens of thousands of copies, and I was about to release the follow-up. For six years I'd been exploring and sharing the principles behind clarity with people who were born into a world where the adults already understood the pre-existing fact of germs. I'd also been sharing my vision of a generation of children being born into a world where the adults already understand the pre-existing fact of the 100% inside-out nature of life.

But all this time, I'd had a secret: while I passionately believed in my vision, and was committed to doing whatever I could to help bring it into being, I'd been afraid to put a deadline on it. The vision already seemed so enormous, so overwhelming, so full of uncertainty... Setting a goal, creating a project and going public with a deadline seemed too big – like an invitation to fail. So I'd been playing it safe; stopping short of what I was inspired to create. And that's when I had a realization...

Your feelings aren't telling you about the risk of failure, the size of the goal or your ability to achieve it...
Your feelings are an experience of the principle of THOUGHT taking form right now, in this moment.

The area where I was feeling *the most* inspired was also the area where my contaminated thinking had seemed most real. The moment I realized this I knew, 'You have to take action and move forward with your goal'.

These principles are to psychology what the discovery of germs was to medicine.
The principles behind clarity represent the future of psychology.
You're going to be exploring and sharing these principles for the next 20 years.

I was remembering my insecurity about the 'Why just 20 years?' question when I had *another* realization. Maybe my insight told me I'd be exploring and sharing these principles for 'the next 20 years' because that's how long it's going to take! I added 20 to 2009, built in a few months of wiggle room, and came up with my goal:

To eradicate chronic psychological suffering globally by 2030

New passion and energy came flooding in. As I started to tell people about the goal, it started taking on a life of its own, and I learned something anew that every great results-creator intuitively understands.

*The creative process is at the heart of how you turn
ideas into reality.*

Many people are confused about how to make things happen, and get stuck making excuses and giving up on their dreams. But when you understand the creative process, you can use it to overcome obstacles and create results that seem extraordinary or even impossible.

There's no such thing as a creative person

There's no such thing as a creative person; there are merely people who have learned how to relate to and be guided by the creative energy of life that's flowing through every human being. The fact that you can see, hear or feel – the fact that you're having an experience right now – means that you're connected to MIND; the creative energy of life. It's creating your experience right now, in this very moment. In fact, the idea 'I'm not creative' is *itself* a creation. If you've been believing that idea until now it's because you've harnessed the creative potential to imagine something about yourself. There's no such thing as a creative person; there are merely people who have learned how to dance with the creative energy of life. The fact that you're reading this means that you have this capacity and you can learn to do this dance.

Who are some of the creators you admire?

Stop for a moment and think about some of the creators or creations you admire. Here are some of my favourites to spark your imagination:

- Elon Musk (founder of Tesla, the electric car company)
- Jane McGonigal (game designer and pioneer)
- Frank Zappa (composer of numerous awesome pieces of music)
- Lady Gaga (multi-talented musician and songwriter)
- Robert Anton Wilson (author of dozens of mind-bending books)
- Barbara Marx Hubbard (visionary futurist)
- Antoni Gaudí (groundbreaking architect)
- Buckminster Fuller (visionary inventor of the geodesic dome)
- JK Rowling (creator of the Harry Potter phenomenon)
- Jonathan Ives (designer of many beautiful Apple products)
- Amanda Palmer (groundbreaking singer, songwriter and author)
- Jimmy White (the most inventive snooker player ever to hold a cue)
- Peter Diamandis (creator of the X-Prize Foundation)
- Lynne Twist (global visionary and social justice campaigner)
- Philippe Petit (highwire artist who did a daring clandestine walk between the twin towers)
- Arianna Huffington (journalist and entrepreneur who created the Huffington Post)
- Tracy Emin (controversial Turner-prize winning artist)
- Adam Curtis (extraordinary documentary maker)
- Daniel Kitson (greatest storyteller I've ever heard)
- Quentin Tarantino (incredible film director)

- Kathy Kolbe (pioneer of the understanding of 'conative strengths')

- You (co-creator of the life you're living)

You see, the people on this list didn't create the things I've mentioned; they *co-created* them. They danced with the creative energy of life to bring those creations into being. Similarly, you've danced with the creative energy of life to co-create the life that you're living. You may say, 'I didn't create it – it just happened to me.' But that's not the case. You are far more creative than you realize. And just as you've danced with life to create the life you're living, you can dance with life to create the results you desire.

It starts with an idea

The creative process begins with an idea, often an authentic desire (something you want just because you want it). The idea often arrives as an insight or realization; it doesn't have to be 'realistic'; its job is to point you in a direction. Remember: your authentic desires are an expression of the infinite intelligence and creative potential that we're all part of; the formless principles of THOUGHT, CONSCIOUSNESS and MIND.

How to deal with resistance

Authentic desires are often (but not always) followed by feelings of insecurity (sometimes referred to as 'resistance'). Here are some of the more common flavours of contaminated thinking that sometimes show up after we get clarity about something we want to create:

- I'm not worthy or deserving of it.

- I don't know how to do it.

- It might not work.

- I'm not good enough.

- I couldn't handle it if people saw me fail.

- I'm not up to the job.
- I don't know where to start.

IMPLICATION: Your conception of the future is not reality; <u>now</u> is reality

As you'll appreciate, 'resistance' is an expression of the outside-in mis-understanding; feelings that are letting you know about THOUGHT taking form in the moment, and nothing else. I was working with a client who was feeling very stuck when they thought about moving forward with a result they wanted to create. They explained that whenever they tried to get started, they felt uncomfortable and got distracted by other activities. I asked them what they thought the feelings were signalling to them: did they believe the feelings were telling them about (a) their future situation, (b) THOUGHT in the moment or (c) a mixture of their thinking and the future situation. They chose (c), a mixture of their thinking and the future situation. This is what I had suspected. While most people are willing to accept that their thinking's got *something* to do with their felt experience, they believe that the future situation (for instance) has got at least *something* to do with it too. But that's not real. 100% of your state of mind is an experience of THOUGHT in the present moment. The future does not yet exist, so none of your felt experience can be coming from the future.

	Solar system	Germ theory	Human experience
A.	A. Sun goes round earth	A. Bad smells cause infection	A. Feelings are letting you know about the future
B.	B. Earth goes round sun	B. Germs cause infection	B. Feelings are letting you know about THOUGHT in the moment and nothing else
C.	C. They take turns	C. A bit of both	C. Feelings are letting you know about a mixture of the future and THOUGHT in the moment

The magical monster stick

When my eldest daughter Tilly was three years old, she became very frightened that monsters would come into her room at night and get her. My efforts to reassure her were to no effect; saying 'there are no monsters, you're perfectly safe' only seemed to make things worse. Finally, I got an idea from a book I was reading. I went out and bought a cool looking 'wand', wrapped it in a silk handkerchief and placed it in a snooker-cue case. I told Tilly that I had something that could solve her monster problem, but it was usually only for bigger girls of five or six. She immediately set to work convincing me that she would be able to handle it. As her mother looked on solemnly, I proceeded to open the snooker-cue case and ceremoniously unveiled the wand from its silk handkerchief. I explained that this was a magical monster stick; that if she waved it three times before she went to sleep, saying 'monsters be gone', her room would be monster-free all night. She practised it while we watched. From that night, her monster problem was gone. Within two weeks, she'd stopped waving the wand. And at some point in the next few months, she realized something a thousand times more valuable than the wand: there's no such thing as monsters; they're just a figment of your imagination.

Understanding that monsters don't exist is infinitely more powerful than monster-repellant.
Understanding the future doesn't exist is infinitely more powerful than resistance-repellant.

Developing your creative process

The prize-winning novelist E.L. Doctorow once said, 'Writing is like driving at night in the fog. You can only see as far as your headlights, but you can make the whole trip that way.' I came across this beautiful quote when I was starting a business in January 2003. I loved what he was pointing to, and used this idea as the basis not only for how I wrote, but for how I developed the company. You see, there are three powerful things implied by this simple quote:

1 *Destination:* you have a 'good enough' sense of the destination you're heading for. You may not know exactly how to get there, and you may not be clear on every single detail of what your destination looks, sounds and feels like, but there's something you know for sure: you have a sense of your destination that's 'good enough' that once you get there, you'll know you've arrived. This mean you're already in a position to begin. You don't need to know what every mile of the journey will look like in detail.

2 *Power:* you have a power source and a means of moving forward. In the case of the car, this includes the engine, driveshaft and wheels, as well as the fuel in your tank. In the case of your life and the results you want to create, the power source is your innate capacities and instincts (the *deep drivers* we explored in Chapters 1 and 6). The fact that you can sense the destination means there's a way for you to move forward.

3 *Navigation:* the combination of your headlights, the instruments on your dashboard and your controls allow you to respond to the ever-changing environment and make adjustments where necessary. Similarly, when you set out to create results, your senses, memories and embodied understanding allow you to use expertise, intuition and sensory data to sense the terrain and respond accordingly.

Remember: you're built for reality. You're capable of so much more than you think you are, and you're better than you realize at responding in the moment. We're all connected to this 'inner guidance system' capable of helping us navigate. When we're caught up in contaminated thinking, we believe we need to 'solve' the resistance before we can move forward, but that's not true. You're capable of more than you think, because you *are* more than you think. As you start moving forward, you will be guided.

How you turn ideas into reality

(1) Take the next step. (2) Calibrate. (3) Repeat… As you step out of La-la Land and move forward in the reality you're built for, the path will emerge before you.

CLARITY plus **ACTION** equals **RESULTS**

Figure 21.1:   The CLARITY® Results Model

> ## Practicality check: How will developing my creative process help me get results?
>
> You're a born results-creator. Contaminated thinking is the most common obstacle to creating results. As you move forward in spite of resistance, you'll discover your own 'flavour' of creation.

As I write, it's been eighteen months since I set my goal to eradicate chronic psychological suffering globally by 2030. As I've kept getting out of my own way and taking the next step, the right people have showed up at the right time. In May 2016, *The World Clarity Foundation* was approved by the UK Charities Commission. Since then, we've appointed the Foundation's Director, Vanessa Pringle. With her guidance, we're testing our assumptions, further defining our aspirations and getting foresight on the practicalities of undertaking a global mission. The process so far has resulted in a powerful vision, mission and purpose for the foundation:

> *The World Clarity Foundation's* purpose is to relieve chronic psychological suffering globally. Our mission is to turn the tide on chronic psychological suffering globally, one person and one community at a time. Our vision is for children to be born into a world where people have a foundational understanding that clarity is the mind's natural state and that innate psychological wellbeing exists within all of us.

The only way we can tackle such an enormous result is using the creative process; using our 'good enough' sense of the destination to guide us in taking the next step, seeing and taking the opportunities that present themselves along the way.

So how do you amplify your results to impact the world on a massive scale?

> **Bottom line results:** Innovation is at the heart of business, and the only sensible response to the rapidly changing business landscape of the twenty-first century. Whether you're a one-man band or leading an enterprise with many thousands of employees, every person in your organization is connected to the creative intelligence of life. The more you're able to utilize the creative intelligence that already exists within your company, the more likely you'll be to prosper in this rapidly changing environment.

> ### *keep exploring ❖ connect with others*
> ### *share your discoveries ❖ deepen your understanding*
>
> **Experiment**: At the end of Chapter 7, I invited you to reflect on some of the results you'd love to create. Now I'd like to invite you to get into action. Choose a result. Do you have a 'good enough' sense of your destination that you'll know it once you get there? What's the very next step you could take towards making it into a reality?
>
> *www.jamiesmart.com/results21*

22

Leveraging Your Results Exponentially

Any company designed for success in the 20th century is doomed to failure in the 21st.

David S. Rose
Author, angel investor, Inc. 500 CEO

'I hate timelines… deadlines… basically I hate all lines… I just want to make all the things… all the time…'

Amanda Palmer's Patreon.com video shows the kimono-clad song-writer using hand-lettered signs to make a request while music from her 2012 album, *Theatre is Evil*, plays in the background. The album was released following a 31-day Kickstarter campaign that raised $1.2 million, but her new video was announcing a much bolder venture. Patreon's MTP (massive transformational purpose) is 'to help every creator in the world achieve a sustainable income'. The platform allows creators to secure pledges from members of their tribes and then collects those pledges on an agreed basis (per month, per song, per work of art etc). The request Palmer makes is simple; she's asking for help. She explains that she wants to make things, and that whether she gets 100 pledges or 10,000, she's going to 'make all the things'. Early in her career, Palmer earned her crust as the Eight Foot Bride, a living statue who offered a flower and a moment of connection to the passers by who put money in the hat at her feet. Today, she continues to innovate, building connection and impact with her audience. Patreon has effectively automated 'the hat', allowing her to get enormous leverage.

Most of us have been conditioned to exchange our time for money, with salaries, day rates and 'charge by the hour' models. But one implication of the commercial transformation can mean transcending this industrial revolution model and discovering new ways to generate value and income. Fortunately, it's never been easier. Digital technology is rapidly transforming the ways we can get leverage. Social technologies have given all of us the kind of communication power historically reserved for governments and only the largest organizations. We all have the tools – now what are you going to do with them? How are you going to use these opportunities to create value?

Innovation gets celebrated; repetition gets automated

Historically, there are two kinds of processes that can create value: *innovation* and *repetition*.

Innovation: innovation involves creating a *new* source of value that didn't exist before. Some examples include writing a novel, building a business, inventing a car, composing a symphony, developing a training programme, designing a video game, creating a perfume, carving a sculpture, architecting a building, developing an app, creating a trusted brand, catalyzing a personal or professional transformation.

Repetition: repetition involves utilizing an *existing* source of value. Some examples include bookkeeping (repeats mathematical functions), an assembly line (repeats mechanical functions), a fast-food chain (repeats food preparation), a supermarket checkout (repeats scanning and selling items), farming (repeats agricultural functions).

A quick look at the existing economy reveals a simple fact about how value already flows...

Innovation gets celebrated.
Repetition gets automated.

Job functions that involve significant amounts of repetition are being automated and/or outsourced. How many jobs that used to be done by a trained employee are now being done by a computer? Here are just a few examples...

- Bank tellers have been replaced by cash points.

- The postal service has been decimated by email.

- Cars that were once built by hand are assembled by robots on 24 × 7 production lines.

- Supermarket checkout clerks are giving way to self-checkout machines.

- High street shops are closing down as retail spend moves to online suppliers.

The rise of the machines

The forward-thinking economist and mathematician Eric Weinstein suggests that the logical extension of the information revolution is this: everything we do based on *human expertise* will eventually be replaced by a computer. The leverage point for value is to move away from 'expertise' and towards a model based on the cultivation of connection, creativity and insight. Once again...

We have to recognize and harness the power of
exponential insight if we want to sense
and respond to the challenges of the digital age.
We have to understand the nature of THOUGHT *if we are to*
survive and thrive as individuals, as organizations, as
societies and as a species.

Strange as it may seem, we're still in the early days of the information revolution. The impact of exponential technology is going to be unimaginably large. For instance...

- According to *Fortune* magazine, a billion women will be joining the global economy by 2020 as entrepreneurs or employees, and will dramatically alter the world of business.

- At least three billion additional people (mostly from Africa, India and China) are due to come online by 2020, with high-speed internet and smartphones. Three billion new minds joining the online economy as consumers, competitors and contributors.

- The emergence of autonomous (driverless) cars is going to profoundly change the transportation landscape. While it may be several decades before they're ubiquitous, current predictions suggest that there will be over 50 million autonomous cars on the roads by 2035.

- There are already sensors in billions of objects (cars, TVs, lights) connecting them to the internet. That's predicted to grow to trillions by 2030. With the rise of the 'internet of everything', virtually *everything* is going to be able to talk to *everything else*, with massive implications for how we live our lives.

- The resulting wearable technology will mean we're able to take more control of our own healthcare, diagnosing illness quickly and accurately. And we're going to be living longer anyway, as we continue to make advances in life extension technology.

- Robots are already being tested in areas where they can go far beyond human limits in terms of precision and accuracy (e.g. eye surgery). The Japanese are also looking to robots as carers and companions to support a large, ageing population.

- Opportunities to leverage community and crowd will only increase, as people become more connected. As virtual technologies continue to improve, the entire planet becomes your talent pool when you're looking to attract the best person for the job.

These powerful drivers are changing the nature of work and how we think about it. So how do you stay relevant in a VUCA world?

Staying relevant in a VUCA world

The Institute for the Future (IFTF) has been producing its annual 10-year forecast for nearly 40 years. The *Future Work Skills 2020* report (produced in 2011) looks at the key skills, abilities and competencies that the workforce of 2020 is going to need in response to the trends referred to above. While some are more obvious than others, all of these 'future-skills' depend on your ability to draw on your *deep drivers*; the innate capacities you were born with. Here's the IFTF list:

IFTF future work skills 2020	Brief definition	Deep drivers/ innate capacities these rely on
Sense-making	The ability to perceive the deeper meaning of situations, and have the insights and realizations necessary for decision making.	Clarity, Creativity, Intuition, Presence
Social intelligence	The ability to be emotionally fluent and connect deeply with others to build strong relationships and collaboration.	Connection, Presence, Authenticity, Intuition
Novel and adaptive thinking	The ability to come up with unique and relevant solutions in unexpected situations.	Clarity, Creativity, Intuition
Cross-cultural competency	The ability to adapt quickly and operate in a variety of contexts and cultures, and as a member of diverse teams.	Connection, Resilience, Presence
Computational thinking	The ability to make decisions based on large data sets, but also to act in the absence of key data.	Intuition, Presence, Clarity
New media literacy	The ability to produce and 'read' video and other new media as fluently as people now produce and read text.	Resilience, Creativity, Intuition
Transdisciplinarity	Literacy in and understanding of multiple fields, in order to solve problems that require multi disciplinary solutions. This requires curiosity and the willingness to keep learning.	Presence, Resilience, Clarity
Design mindset	Organizing your approach, environment and thinking to support different kinds of tasks and outcomes.	Presence, Creativity, Direction
Cognitive load management	The ability to deal with the increasing barrage of information, being strategically selective about what is and isn't given attention.	Clarity, Resilience
Virtual collaboration	The ability to be productive, engage others and (potentially) to lead others as part of a virtual team.	Presence, Connection, Clarity, Direction

Reality check

'Hang on a minute', you may be thinking. 'After reading this chapter, I'm starting to get properly freaked out by the rapid rate of technological change. How is *that* going to help me get exponential results?' Remember: you can't be a victim of circumstance. Freaked out feelings are *only* ever letting you know about THOUGHT in the moment; not about technology, your skills or the future.

In a world where new technologies, platforms and engagement models are emerging every month, the illusion that we can look to the external world to provide a sense of security and stability is no longer viable. That sense of security and stability can *only* come from within. As you deepen your understanding of the principles behind clarity, and your sense of inner security continues to increase, you'll find yourself experiencing more and more freedom to experiment.

The power of experimenting

In their book *Art & Fear: Observations on the Perils (and Rewards) of Artmaking*, David Bayles and Ted Orland tell the story of a ceramics teacher who divided their class into two groups. The first group were told they would be graded on the *quantity* of pots they made, while the second group were told they'd be graded on their pots' *quality*. At the end of term, it emerged that the finest pots were produced by the 'quantity' group. Why? Because while the 'quality' group were agonizing over how to create the perfect pot, the 'quantity' group were experimenting, making countless pots, learning from their mistakes, and improving in the process.

Practicality check: How is exponential leverage going to help me get results?

The technologies you need to exponentially leverage your results *already exist*, and new ones are being created every day. You have the ability to learn about them, use them and experiment with them. In fact, the only thing that *ever* stops people from learning and experimenting is contaminated thinking, showing up as fear: fear of failure, fear of criticism, fear of the unknown, fear of change, fear of loss etc. When we cling to an outdated model of the world, we may enjoy the temporary comfort of the familiar. But all the while, the gap between the model and reality is continuing to increase. And the bigger the gap, the greater the risk, and the more demanding the 'update' when it happens (remember what happened to the fortunes of the music business, the hotel trade and London's black cabs?). You live in a world of opportunity. Exponential results come from insight, experimentation and action.

Every experiment is an opportunity for learning.
And while they may not always turn out the way you expect
them to, experiments always get results.

CLARITY   plus   **ACTION**   equals   **RESULTS**

Figure 22.1:   The CLARITY® Results Model

At the time of writing (2016), Amanda Palmer's Patreon channel showed 7964 patrons pledging to pay $35,984 for each 'thing' she produces (an average of $4.52 per patron per thing). She inspires a loyalty in her audience that is based on authenticity, transparency and genuine connection.

So how do you create the kind of transformational experiences your audience desires?

Bottom line results: The world of work is changing rapidly. Job functions that involve significant amounts of repetition are being automated and/or outsourced, while new value is being created through the cultivation of connection, creativity and insight. With new ways of working come the need for new skills and qualities. As the demand for these skills continues to increase, the prizes will go to the individuals and organizations who manage to leverage their innate capacities and instincts. Creativity, perceptiveness and social intelligence underpin the work skills that are going to be essential in 2020 and beyond.

keep exploring ⁑ connect with others
share your discoveries ⁑ deepen your understanding

Experiment: An experiment is something you create in order to test an idea, so what's an idea you'd like to test? What's an experiment you can perform to test that idea? Design it, test it and learn from your results.

www.jamiesmart.com/results22

23

The Key to Creating Transformational Experiences

Long experience has taught me that the crux of my fortunes is whether I can radiate good will toward my audience. There is only one way to do it and that is to feel it. You can fool the eyes and minds of the audience, but you cannot fool their hearts.

Howard Thurston
Magician

'Do you want to know the biggest leverage point for improving the quality of your customers' experience?'

I was having an initial meeting with the general manager of a luxury hotel, and the subject of TripAdvisor ratings had come up. The site's user-generated reviews have a big influence on the hospitality industry, and one of his objectives was to get the hotel into the top 10 for his city. He told me about the obstacles he was up against: high turnover among millennials, increasingly demanding customers, changes in buying habits driven by new technology. He talked about the results he wanted to achieve: a stronger brand, higher engagement and productivity, attracting, retaining and developing the best talent. When I asked him my question, he looked slightly amused and invited me to tell him. 'The biggest leverage point for improving the quality of your customers' experience is the quality of the experience you and your team are having'. He looked shocked, and said he agreed. He told me that he passionately believed this, but that I was one of the only people he'd ever met who held the same view. I asked him what he'd tried, and he told me about a variety of efforts to build a stronger, happier team. Some had worked well, while others had not. Some people had been impacted, while others were unaffected. I said I understood, and asked, 'Do you want to know the single biggest influence on the quality of you and your team's experience?' He did.

> *Your understanding of how your experience is created*
> *is the ultimate leverage point for improving the*
> *quality of that experience.*
> *The more deeply you understand the principles behind*
> *clarity, the more you benefit from your mind's ability to*
> *self-correct to resilience, creativity and connection.*

Whether you call it the 'connection economy', the 'transformation economy' or the 'experience economy', clients and customers want results. Expectations are increasing – high-quality products and services are the minimum requirement, and people want them now. So how do you create the kind of transformational experiences that lead to great reviews, valuable referrals and raving fans? It turns out that the most powerful leverage point for impactful customer experiences is *inside the mind of the customer*. The only place value can *ever* be created is in the mind of the audience. Value is in the mind of the beholder, and is an emergent property of the relationship. And where all the elements of value come together is in the customer experience.

The fish rots from the head down

Remember the *Harvard Business Review* article showing that leaders' states of mind are 'transmitted' to other people? This is not a new observation; an ancient proverb captures the infectious nature of contaminated thinking in the phrase, 'the fish rots from the head down'. But it turns out that the same infectious quality is true of the calm, happy, energized states that drive high performance, connection and positive experiences. Companies that are renowned for the quality of their *customers*' experiences (e.g. Apple, Google, Southwest Airlines, Zappos) recognize the fact that it's correlated to their *employees*' experiences.

Figure 23.1:   The CLARITY® Culture Model

Leading management and business thinker Peter Drucker famously remarked that 'culture eats strategy for breakfast'. So what exactly is the culture of a company, a community or a society?

Culture is the expression of a group's level of consciousness; their collective clarity of understanding.
And the thoughts, words, actions and artefacts that make sense from that level of understanding.

While there will be various *expressions* of that level of understanding (e.g. stories, rituals, values, procedures, habits of thinking, beliefs, organization charts, metrics, rules, awards, celebrations), the thing that *drives* them is the level of consciousness behind them. As an organization's collective clarity of understanding increases, things that used to be normal stop making sense, and things that used to seem impossible are suddenly sensible and straightforward.

The day-to-day expression of a group's level of understanding determines the collective state of mind it operates from. This affects numerous important factors, all of which correlate to the deep drivers we've been exploring, including...

- Clarity of purpose, direction and communication to stakeholders (e.g. TED's purpose – to spread ideas – is known by millions of people, and reflects a clarity of direction and communication that has transformed the organization).

- How resilient and agile the employees and organization are in their ability to respond (e.g. Apple teams sometimes look more like a startup than part of a billion-dollar company, working independently on key projects).

- How willing to experiment, risk failing and celebrate the insights gained in the process (e.g. Google regularly gives awards for the biggest failed experiment that yielded the biggest *insight*).

- How creative the organization is in solving problems and innovating (e.g. design firm IDEO are using their OpenIDEO platform to leverage a large global community, crowdsourcing solutions to some of the world's biggest challenges).

- The sense of genuine connection to each other, and to the community they serve (e.g. digital media company, Gimlet Media, transparently showcases its culture and builds connection with its audience through the podcasts it creates).

- The 'feel' of the brand, and the feeling state experienced by employees and customers alike (e.g. every brand you've ever had an experience of, and every company you've ever interacted with... for better or worse).

Here's a simple way of thinking about it...

Contamination days: you know those days when it probably would have been better if you'd stayed under the duvet... Where nothing seems to turn out right, and it's almost as if you're working against yourself... And it's stressful and unproductive... And everything seems like a struggle and a chore... And you finish the day wondering where it went, with nothing to show for it but a headache and more on your to-do list.

Clarity days: and then there are those other days when you can't seem to put a foot wrong, and everything's falling into place... Those days when it's almost as if you're being guided, and you're unusually productive... Feeling at ease, yet focused... Coming up with great ideas, and finding solutions easily... And you finish the day with a sense of accomplishment, feeling fulfilled and satisfied with a job well done.

The kind of day a person is having determines whether they're showing up as a plus or a minus in their organization. And while most of us have both of these kinds of days from time to time, their frequency and duration is a function of your clarity of understanding. As you get a deeper understanding of the principles behind clarity, you'll find yourself having fewer 'contamination days' and more 'clarity days'. Perhaps best of all, the self-correcting nature of the mind means that even if you start out having a bad day, it can turn into a clarity day in a heartbeat, because...

The thing that transforms your experience from contamination to clarity is a realization... an insight... a fresh new thought.
And you're <u>wired</u> for insight, because you're built for reality... Optimized for success, with the factory settings for creating results.

The deeper your understanding of the principles behind clarity, the more easily you'll find yourself defaulting to the factory settings.

Reality Check

'Are you saying that if everyone in my company is in a good mood, then our customers will be too? That seems like cloud cuckoo land!' I'm not saying that. Your clients and customers are paying for the results that matter to them. But their *experience* is going to depend on more than just the results they get or the transformation they go through; it's also going to be a function of the way they *feel*. As we head towards a trillion-sensor world, and see virtual technologies being used to create blended realities (where the digital world is blended with the physical world), companies will have more and more influence over the external and internal aspects of a person's experience. But, as I wrote in my first book, *CLARITY*...

The value of an event is dependent on the quality of the experience the person has. The quality of the experience a person has is 100% dependent on their level of clarity when they're having the experience. This is why understanding the nature of THOUGHT is so fundamental to the experience economy.

Of course customers are paying for the results that matter to them. High-quality products and services are now expected as standard. But here's the thing: you can go to the best restaurant in the world. It doesn't matter how good the restaurant is, how good the service is or how good the food is; if you don't have a great *experience*, it's likely to get a one out of five on TripAdvisor.

By the same token, you can go to a restaurant that *isn't* so great; where the food is so-so, or the service leaves something to be desired. But if you have a great *experience*, chances are you're going to give it a good rating. Remember:

Your customer's feelings are giving them feedback about the 'glasses' they're wearing, not who or what they're looking at. Their experience will be consistent with their level of clarity in the moment.

The customer's experience always comes from THOUGHT in the moment. If they're in a bad state of mind, they'll tend to blame it on the restaurant, the food or the people they're with. No matter how good the service, they'll find something to take issue with. No matter how exquisite the meal, it won't be up to scratch. Conversely, if they're in a good state of mind, then they're likely to attribute it to the food, the restaurant and the people they're with. If they're in a good feeling, they'll be more likely to overlook or forgive poor service, bland food or drab decor.

Of course, if the service, food and decor are first-class *and* your customers are in a good feeling, you're on track for a five-star review.

How to turn a one-star circumstance into a five-star experience

So what's going to have the biggest influence on the 'glasses' your customers are wearing? The 'glasses' you and your employees are wearing. Moods are infectious, but clarity of understanding is a powerful inoculator. As you deepen your understanding of the inside-out nature of life, you'll be less likely to 'catch' the negative moods of your colleagues and customers, and be more capable of leading them in a positive direction. And here's the thing: mistakes may still happen from time to time, but your ability to respond from a place of resilience, connection and clarity is the thing most likely to turn a situation around, and put a smile on a customer's face. That's how you turn a one-star circumstance into a five-star experience.

Case Study: The power of experimentation

In Chapter 9, I told you about Pete Bryceland, who responded to an email from me asking 'Would you like me to collaborate with you on growing your business?' What I didn't mention was that the email was the first part of an experiment I was conducting. I'd noticed that many self-employed transformation professionals (coaches, trainers, consultants, nutritionists, therapists etc) struggled with the commercial aspects of their work, and I had a hypothesis: if I were to teach them the principles behind clarity, while taking them through the three transformations we're exploring here (grounding, impact and leverage), it would have a significant effect on their wellbeing, their impact and their income. I wanted to test the hypothesis, so I sent out the email above to some of the members of my tribe who had previously indicated they were transformation professionals. This was the first part of the experiment.

The second part of the experiment was the email conversations that kicked off after Pete and a number of other people responded positively. As we emailed back and forth, I was *learning*; gathering high-quality information about my audience. I was 'getting' their world, and as I did, the programme I'd had in mind started to come into sharper focus. 'What are your aspirations for the year ahead? What have you tried so far to get these results? What do you think the sticking points have been?' Despite the constrained nature of the email format, my focus throughout was on connecting with and serving my prospective client.

The third part of the experiment came at a certain point in the conversation, when I felt I had a good sense of what Pete was up against, and what he would need to get the results he wanted. I replied to his latest email, asking if he would like to take part in an experimental project I was conducting. This was the first time I'd outlined my hypothesis to a prospective client, and Pete was interested. He had some questions about the investment of time and money, and when I told him what I had in mind, he replied, 'OK I'm in!'.

Now came the fourth part of the experiment; designing the programme. I reflected deeply on the question, 'How can you help your clients get the results they desire, and have an amazing experience in the process?' I outlined the different elements, and designed the kind of programme *I* would have wanted when I was in their shoes. We gathered a group of clients to go through the 'beta test' phase of the programme and began. The beta test group included people joining me live in London, and live-streaming from around the world. It was a 12-week journey, and people like Pete saw profound transformations in their personal lives and their professional results.

We decided to run the programme a second time, and that's when some-thing unexpected started to happen. Remember: a tribe is a group of people whose values and world view are similar enough that they find it easy to connect with and relate to each other. We started to build an audience, a tribe of transformation professionals whose values and world views are very similar to each other. Eighteen months later, hundreds of transformation professionals have been through the programme, and the tribe is stronger than ever.

It wouldn't have happened if I hadn't done the first experiment, and sent Pete that email. Through my conversations with Pete and a num-ber of other transformation professionals, I was able to get closer to this audience; to get clear on what their problems, needs, wants and desires were. That enabled me to design a solution that would help them *get* those results. It also allowed me to test whether the solution I'd designed was viable, *before* I went away and built it. As a result, the experience we've been able to create is a reflection of what matters most to me and my team, and focuses on delivering what matters most to our clients.

Practicality check: How are transformational experiences going to help me get results?

In Chapter 20, we looked at what people pay for: the transformations they desire, the stories that reflect their values, the results they want to create and the way they want to feel. 'Customer experience' is another way of saying 'how people feel while they're experiencing your product/service/company/brand'. 100% of the customer experience comes from THOUGHT taking form in the moment. These days, high-quality products and services are expected; your biggest leverage point is your clients' *experience* of what you offer. The most powerful way to influence that is through the experience you and your team are having. And the most powerful way to influence *that* is your understanding of the principles behind clarity.

| CLARITY | equals | CAPACITY | minus | CONTAMINATION |

Figure 23.2:   The CLARITY® Equation

So now that you know the key to transformational experiences, how do you prosper in the transformation economy?

Bottom line results: Companies that are renowned for the quality of their *customers'* experiences recognize that they're correlated to the quality of their *employees'* experiences. The kind of day a person is having determines whether they're showing up as a plus or a minus in your organization. The kinds of days the people in your organization have are an expression of the *clarity of understanding* of those people. Another word for this is 'culture'. Culture is the expression of a group's level of consciousness; their collective clarity of understanding, and the thoughts, words, actions and artefacts that make sense from that level of understanding. If you want to increase the number of 'plus' days in your organization, your biggest leverage point is an increase in clarity of understanding.

keep exploring ❖ connect with others
share your discoveries ❖ deepen your understanding

Experiment: Start looking out for the link between state of mind and the quality of experience a person is having. Before long, you should start to notice a strong correlation between the two. You might even notice the effect that one person's state of mind can *appear* to have on someone else's state of mind. Of course, it all works from the inside-out. Nobody can 'make you' feel a certain way (even though it sometimes seems as though they can). The only thing that can give you a feeling is THOUGHT in the moment. Isn't that nice to know?

www.jamiesmart.com/results23

24

Prospering in the Transformation Economy

....

A new type of thinking is essential if mankind is to survive and move toward higher levels.

Albert Einstein
Physicist, winner of the Nobel Prize in
Physics, 1921

'I came to the conclusion that we should aspire to increase the scope and scale of human consciousness in order to better understand what questions to ask. Really, the only thing that makes sense is to strive for greater collective enlightenment...'

Elon Musk's statement shocked me. Greater collective enlightenment? Musk is one of the founders of PayPal; the creator of Tesla Motors, SpaceX and Solar City. He was the inspiration for the screen persona of Tony Stark, the whisky-swilling, billionaire playboy engineer-turned-superhero in the *Iron Man* films. Then suddenly, it all fell into place... Just as he'd used PayPal as a stepping stone to fund Tesla (electric cars), SpaceX (space exploration) and Solar City (solar energy), these three ventures are in service of a much larger vision: ending our reliance on fossil fuels, solving the global warming problem and making humanity a multi-planetary species (one of Musk's aims is to start a colony on Mars). To what end? Musk's purpose is the evolution of human consciousness. He's using technology, insight and action to succeed where governments and legacy industries are failing. In the process, he and his team are disrupting the status quo, with remarkable results. His companies attract top talent; purpose-driven high performers exhilarated by the chance to make a difference in the world. The factories rely on advanced robotics to build automobiles, space vehicles and solar power cells. The fleet of Tesla cars is a 'learning network', leveraging sensors, wireless connectivity and artificial intelligence to collect and make sense of vast amounts of data. With every mile travelled, the fleet gets smarter, and the domain of driverless cars gets closer.

The exponential nature of technology is transforming our world at an ever-increasing pace. Robots are becoming more versatile and artificial intelligence is becoming more commonplace. According to MIT Sloan School of Management professor Erik Brynjolfsson and his collaborator Andrew McAfee (co-authors of the book *Race Against the Machine*) repetitive jobs are being automated more quickly than new jobs are being created. As computing power continues to get faster and cheaper, whole categories of employment are likely to disappear. The jobs at the highest risk of automation are those involving repetitive tasks and expertise that can be specified and codified. The jobs at the lowest risk of automation are those requiring high degrees of perceptiveness, creativity and social intelligence. There's an obvious conclusion you can draw from this...

> *The capacities you need to prosper in the twenty-first century can be summarized as perceptiveness, creativity and social intelligence.*

The data shown in Figure 24.1 have been 'cherry-picked' from a list of over 700 jobs spread across the range from low probability of computerization to high probability. This has been done (a) for reasons of brevity and (b) to shine a light on the extremes, highlighting the jobs with the lowest and highest risk of automation.

Perceptiveness, creativity and social intelligence

Many professions which we may not ordinarily think of as having these qualities are actually rich in them, for instance...

- Scientists and engineers need to be able to think creatively to solve problems.

- Trial lawyers need to have a high degree of social intelligence to influence judges and juries (and public opinion, in some cases).

- Surgeons need to be perceptive, thinking systemically and working with high levels of manual dexterity to operate successfully on a patient.

NB: the fine motor skills required to perform surgery are another thing that can be particularly difficult to automate. However, Oxford University has recently agreed to run human clinical trials

Probability that jobs will be eliminated as a result of innovations in digital technology (including computerization, robotics and artificial intelligence)

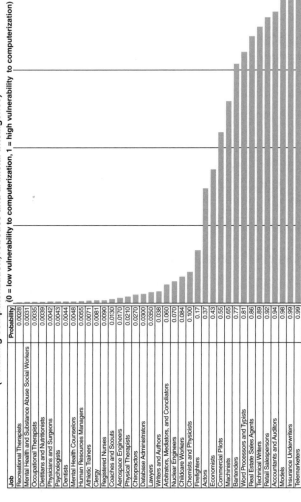

(0 = low vulnerability to computerization, 1 = high vulnerability to computerization)

Job	Probability
Recreational Therapists	0.0028
Mental Health and Substance Abuse Social Workers	0.0031
Occupational Therapists	0.0035
Dietitians and Nutritionists	0.0039
Physicians and Surgeons	0.0042
Psychologists	0.0043
Dentists	0.0044
Mental Health Counselors	0.0048
Human Resources Managers	0.0055
Athletic Trainers	0.0071
Clergy	0.0081
Registered Nurses	0.0090
Coaches and Scouts	0.0130
Aerospace Engineers	0.0170
Physical Therapists	0.0210
Chiropractors	0.0270
Database Administrators	0.0300
Lawyers	0.0350
Writers and Authors	0.038
Arbitrators, Mediators, and Conciliators	0.060
Nuclear Engineers	0.070
Childcare Workers	0.084
Chemists and Physicists	0.100
Firefighters	0.17
Actors	0.37
Economists	0.43
Commercial Pilots	0.55
Machinists	0.65
Bartenders	0.77
Word Processors and Typists	0.81
Real Estate Sales Agents	0.86
Technical Writers	0.89
Retail Salespersons	0.92
Accountants and Auditors	0.94
Models	0.98
Insurance Underwriters	0.99
Telemarketers	0.99

Source: THE FUTURE OF EMPLOYMENT: HOW SUSCEPTIBLE ARE JOBS TO COMPUTERISATION? by Carl Benedikt Frey and Michael A. Osborne, 2013

Figure 24.1:   Susceptibility of Jobs to Exponential Technologies of PRECEYES, a system for robot-assisted eye surgery that will give surgeons an unparalleled degree of precision.

The rise of the transformation professional

A large number of the jobs at an extremely *low* risk of automation involve *transformation professionals* (e.g. psychologists, clergy, physicians, nutritionists, coaches); roles where bedside manner counts, and much of the value is created through connection, creativity and insight. The 'wellbeing industry' is growing by leaps and bounds, and the past decade has seen hundreds of thousands of people drawn to the 'profession of transformation'. As our global consciousness continues to rise, industries are disrupted and working patterns change. More and more people are seeking greater independence and freedom. We're being drawn to values-based, purpose-driven work that utilizes our gifts and passions. And when it comes to perceptiveness, creativity and social intelligence, there's something important you need to know...

You're already connected to the source of creativity
and innovation.
You're already optimized to thrive as a socially
intelligent being.
You're already endowed with the powers of perceptiveness
and persuasion.

You already have these capacities. They're as integral to your nature as your ability to see, hear or feel. The only thing that slows your development or gets in the way is contaminated thinking, arising from the outside-in misunderstanding. The reason people have struggled to teach these 'emotional intelligences' until now is because they've been trying to do it using *additive* approaches. But remember: embodied understanding is *subtractive*. As your understanding of the principles behind clarity continues to increase, your capacities for creativity, perceptiveness and social intelligence automatically come to the fore.

CLARITY   equals   **CAPACITY**   minus   **CONTAMINATION**

Figure 24.2:   The CLARITY® Equation

Clarity of understanding gives rise to the qualities you need to thrive, prosper and create meaningful results in the twenty-first century.

Reality check

So am I saying there's nothing else to learn? That if you deepen your understanding of these principles, you'll automatically know how to develop a mobile app, master the latest social media tools and play the guitar like Jimi Hendrix? Of course not – that's a ridiculous notion. As the rate of innovation continues to increase, there are new skills to learn and tools to master. Whether it's 'soft skills' such as selling and negotiating or 'hard skills' such as software development and data science, there are some things in life that are responsive to instruction, practise and mastery. You wouldn't want to travel in a plane flown by a pilot who had never been to flight school and was just 'trusting their intuition'. But by the same token, you wouldn't want to travel in a plane flown by a pilot who was highly skilled and experienced, but who was lost in an outside-in La-la Land ruminating over a pay dispute. And that's the key: As you get a deeper understanding of the principles behind clarity, you *automatically* benefit from your innate capacities, and increase your bandwidth and selectivity for learning the skills and capabilities that *aren't* innate. Your ability to create results relies both on your innate capacities, and on the skills and abilities they enable you to learn.

Closing the gap

The philosopher Gregory Bateson wisely pointed out that 'The major problems in the world are the result of the difference between how nature works and the way people think'.

You can view the evolution of human knowledge and understanding as a process of closing the gap between how reality already works and the way we believe it works.

The closing of that gap is a reflection of the increase in our collective level of consciousness; humanity's clarity of understanding. And as humanity's level of consciousness continues to rise, we see the external expressions of that evolution...

- The infant mortality rate has declined dramatically over the past 100 years.

- Rates of murder and other violence continue to fall; we live at the most peaceful time in human history.

- Billions of people are able to communicate with each other.

- The number of countries adopting democratic systems continues to increase.

- Tolerance and acceptance of alternative lifestyles is on the rise.

- People are demanding greater transparency, authenticity and integrity from businesses.

- Companies are scrabbling to bring more 'emotional intelligence' into the workplace.

- More and more people are inspired to do values-based, purpose-driven work.

The move towards greater independence, freedom and purpose is an expression of this increase in humanity's clarity of understanding.

Remember, for practical purposes, you have the ability to perceive yourself as distinct and separate from the rest of life. But you are never *actually* separate. You are inseparable from the intelligence and oneness of life, part of an undivided whole. I invite you to open to the possibility that the reason so many people are seeking values-based, purpose-driven work is because our collective consciousness is continuing to rise.

Case Study: What would you do if it was OK to fail?

Over 29,000 people follow Christina's Instagram feed where she posts recipes and photos of the delicious, nourishing meals she prepares. Christina is passionate about nutrition, but by day she works as an auditor. She had just put up her new website, and was getting enquiries from potential clients wanting to work with her, but she had a problem. Christina had been hit by a paralysing mix of emotions. She suddenly doubted her ability to do the work she loved, and was gripped by 'fraud' feelings, with a sense of unworthiness and 'who am I to do this?' She comes from a very traditional family, and her parents don't understand how she could make a living by following her passion. They're concerned for her security and wellbeing, and want her to stick with something 'safe', like her current job. Christina was terrified at the thought of failure, and of disappointing her parents, so she asked me for help. In the midst of our conversation, I asked a standard 'coaching question'...

Jamie: What would you do if you couldn't fail?
Christina: I'd do it. I'd become a nutritionist.
Jamie: Great. Here's a slightly different question. What would you do if it was OK to fail?
Christina: Same thing. I'd become a nutritionist.
Jamie: Great. That means the only issue you've <u>actually</u> had is that you didn't realize that it's <u>OK</u> to fail.

Failure is a concept; it doesn't exist in *reality*. Every time you do an experiment, you get a result. It may not be the result you wanted, but you can learn from it and feed that learning into the next experiment. I said, 'You weren't born with a fear of failure, otherwise you would never have learned to walk or talk'. And like learning to walk and talk, success in a new enterprise is almost always built on a foundation of numerous experiments (at least some of which fail to achieve the desired resilts). That's part of the nature of learning.

Christina said she understood, but that she still felt worried and anxious at the thought of making a mistake and disappointing her parents. After exploring this with her for a few minutes, I said. . .

You're feeling THOUGHT in this moment, not the future
or other people's opinions.
Your feelings are giving you feedback on the glasses you're
wearing, not what you're thinking about.

We looked up 'nutritionist' on Frey and Osborne's chart (see above figure) and found it at number 11 (with a score of 0.0039) meaning they'd evaluated it as among the *least* likely of all jobs to be computerized. According to Frey and Osborne's research, when it comes to the risk of computerization, being a dietician or a nutritionist is one of the safest jobs there is. We then looked up Christina's current job role, 'auditor'. Frey and Osborne had scored it as a 0.94, meaning it was among the *most* likely of all jobs to be computerized.

Christina sat silently for a few moments as she realized that the jobs her parents considered *safest* were actually among the *most* vulnerable to computerization and elimination. The job that looked the most *dangerous* to them was actually one of the *least* vulnerable. She told me that the firm she worked for was already planning redundancies, and that she'd been looking for another auditing job so she could 'play it safe'.

Christina's passion for nutrition, combined with her willingness to experiment with social media, mean that she is well-placed to prosper in the transformation economy. The education system has trained her for a world of work that will soon disappear, so there are new things for her to learn. But if she's willing to go through the three transformations we're exploring in this book, and continue experimenting, she has every reason to be hopeful.

Steam-engine-time

Charles Fort famously wrote 'A tree cannot find out, as it were, how to blossom, until comes blossom-time. A social growth cannot find out the use of steam engines, until comes steam-engine-time'. Science fiction writers use the phrase 'steam-engine-time' to describe the phenomenon of a large number of writers independently coming up with the same idea at roughly the same point. There are a variety of explanations for why the steam engine (and countless other innovations) arrived when they did. These range from their reliance on the development of supporting innovations and inventions through to the development of the concepts, ideas and social structures. But there's another possibility...

As we continue closing the gap between how reality already
works and the way we believe it works, we discover new
problems to be solved, and new opportunities
to be developed.
As our collective level of consciousness continues to increase,
MIND *– the intelligence behind life – brings what the world*
needs into being through us.

Reality check

'Hang on a second! We may be living at the least violent time in history, but aren't stress, anxiety and depression on the increase?' Yes and no. In their book *The Third Wave*, Alvin and Heidi Toffler describe the waves of transformation that have swept the planet over the past 10,000 years. Each wave was the result of a certain 'leverage point'; an aspect of reality that was *already true*, but that hadn't been realized (insightfully understood) until that point in history. The Tofflers specified the first three waves (Agricultural, Industrial and Information), but we're now seeing the rise of the fourth wave, The Thought Revolution. As each wave rises, existing problems are solved, benefits are realized and new problems are created. Solutions to the new problems are delivered by the next wave, for example:

Transformation	Leverage point	Examples of problems solved/Benefits created	Examples of new problems/ Challenges created
The Agricultural Revolution (first wave – circa 8000 BC)	Understanding of farming and agriculture	– Massively stabilized food supply – Ability to settle territory – Ability to create goods – Writing	– Harder work for some – Inequality/slave labour – Increased risk of disease
The Industrial Revolution (second wave – circa 1760)	Understanding of mechanization/ industry	– Improved transportation – More and better goods – Increased standard of living	– Pollution/environmental damage – Migration/disrupted families – Industrial-scale warfare

(Continued)

Transformation	Leverage point	Examples of problems solved/Benefits created	Examples of new problems/Challenges created
The Information Revolution (third wave – circa 1940)	Understanding of information/ digitization/ computerization	– Improved communication and access to information (facilitated the 'Arab Spring' uprising and the increase in democracy globally) – Dematerialization of goods (smartphones mean you can have a phone, camera, satnav, torch, stereo and numerous other devices in your pocket) – Increased automation	– Technological unemployment – Information overwhelm – Attention poverty – Time scarcity – Mental congestion – Connection starvation – Increasing volatility, uncertainty, complexity and ambiguity – Increases in stress, anxiety and depression
The Thought Revolution (fourth wave – in progress)	Understanding of the nature of THOUGHT	– Reduced stress, anxiety and depression – Deeper connection to self, others and life as a whole – Greater clarity, wellbeing and peace of mind – Higher performance – More intuition, creativity and innovation – More valuable innovations – Increased social intelligence – Improved mental health – Greater wisdom in business, governments and other institutions – Resolution of long-standing social problems, (many of which have bedeviled humanity for millennia)	?

'So are you saying all we need is to understand the principles behind clarity, and all our problems will disappear? That I'll suddenly be able to create exponential results and live the life of my dreams?' I'm not saying that. We live at a pivotal point in history. While in many ways, things are better than ever, we also face some of the biggest threats yet to our existence as a species, including climate change, artificial intelligence, radical fundamentalism and poverty.

In September 2015, the United Nations announced a set of 17 Sustainable Development Goals (SDGs) with the aim of massively transforming the quality of life for *all* life on the planet. Here is a summarized version of the SDGs:

- End poverty everywhere
- End hunger and improve nutrition
- Ensure good health and wellbeing
- Ensure quality education for all
- Achieve gender equality
- Clean water and sanitation for all
- Affordable and clean energy for all
- Decent work and economic growth
- Industry, innovation and infrastructure
- Reduce inequality
- Safe, sustainable cities and settlements
- Sustainable production and consumption
- Combat climate change
- Conserve oceans and marine resources
- Protect and sustain life on land
- Peace, justice and strong institutions
- Partnerships for achieving these goals

The SDGs represent massively transformational results for the whole of humanity. A quick analysis will reveal that the achievement of these goals will be the result of the level of consciousness of the people involved in them, and the actions that level of consciousness inspires.

Our collective clarity of understanding is the ultimate leverage point for creating results in our own lives, and for all of humanity.

Transforming negative VUCA to positive VUCA

Futurist and former president of the Institute for the Future (IFTF), Bob Johansen, suggests that there's a counterpoint to the often overwhelming 'negative VUCA' of Volatility, Uncertainty, Complexity and Ambiguity; the 'positive VUCA' of Vision, Understanding, Clarity and Agility. And what transforms negative VUCA into positive VUCA?

Foresight… Insight… Realization…

The IFTF creates scenarios to give leaders 'foresight'; a 'feel' for possible futures. As leaders reflect on these future scenarios, they often have insights and realizations relating both to the present, and to the way forward. In the face of insight, volatility inspires vision, uncertainty resolves to understanding, ambiguity gives way to agility and complexity yields to clarity.

Figure 24.3:   Negative VUCA plus Insight equals Positive VUCA

In times of transformational change, it's easy to be comforted by the opiates of habit, tradition and business-as-usual. It takes courage to step into the unknown, and tread purposefully in the domain of experiment, exploration and transformation. So I'll tell you what I often tell my clients at the start of my one-year programmes…

On the one hand, I want you to be wildly successful,
whatever your definition of success turns out to be…
And on the other hand, I want you to become the fullest
expression of who you really are.

*Because it turns out that becoming the fullest
expression of who you really are...
Is the surest path to becoming wildly successful...
Whatever your definition of success turns out to be.*

Practicality check: How is understanding the transformation economy going to help me get results?

We're right at the start of the most disruptive phase in human history; the challenges we face are significant. As Einstein said, if mankind is to survive and move towards higher levels, it will come as a result of actions born from a *new* type of thinking; an increase in our individual and collective consciousness.

CLARITY   plus   **ACTION**   equals   **RESULTS**

Figure 24.4:   The CLARITY® Results Model

We're all on this journey together, hurtling through space at 67,000 miles per hour. The fact that you're reading this book means that you're already increasing your understanding of the principles behind clarity. As you get a deeper embodied understanding of how the mind already works, *who you really are* will be showing up more and more of the time. This is the path to the kind of results worth creating, and the kind of success worth having.

Bottom line results: Perceptiveness, creativity and social intelligence are key to business prosperity in the next 20 years. People already have these capacities; the only thing that slows development or gets in the way is contaminated thinking. Remember: embodied understanding is subtractive. As your understanding of the principles behind clarity continues to increase, your capacities for creativity, perceptiveness and social intelligence automatically come to the fore.

keep exploring ∻ connect with others
share your discoveries ∻ deepen your understanding

Experiment: At the beginning of this book, I asked you a question: What's the number one result that – if you were to achieve it – you believe would have the biggest positive impact in your life? Ask yourself this question again, or get someone else to ask you. It can be fun to compare your answer now to the answer you gave when you first started this book. How have your perspectives changed? What are some of your more liberating insights and realizations since reading the book? Are you open to the possibility that your authentic desires are an expression of a deeper intelligence; of humanity's collective consciousness? What are some of the things you're inspired to do, create or become, moving forward?

www.jamiesmart.com/results24

Acknowledgements

My heartfelt thanks and appreciation go to...

All my teachers, colleagues and clients, past and present.

The pioneering community of Clarity coaches, consultants, trainers and practitioners who are with me on this adventure.

The people who have so generously allowed me to tell their stories in this book: Ani, Ankush, Christina, Donna, Ian, Jim, Jo, John, Juan, Katherine, Mahima, Mamoon, Marina, Pete, Tallulah, Tilly and the Council of the Institute and Faculty of Actuaries.

Patrick Cumiskey, for introducing me to the fighter within.

Dean Jackson, for more cheese and less whiskers.

Joe Gregory, for helping bring order out of chaos.

Michael Perez, for your excellent feedback and pain relief.

John Epstein, for the wonderful connection quotation and everything else.

Tom Oxford Smith, for your collaboration, patience and beautiful artwork.

The team at Capstone, for your support and expertise.

Robin Charbit and Ken Manning, PhD, for your wisdom, simplicity and encouragement.

Sandy Krot, for your wisdom and the story about President Garfield's assassination.

Michael Neill, for your friendship, your insight into my direction and for patiently pointing me towards these principles.

Dicken Bettinger, Keith Blevens PhD, Cathy Casey, Chip Chipman, Mark Howard PhD, Rita Shuford, Cheryl Bond and Jan Chipman and for your friendship, guidance and mentorship on the *Clarity Trainer Training Programme*.

Joanne Nicholls, for all the learning, friendship and good times.

Chantal Burns, for your love, fun and invaluable feedback.

Garret Kramer, for your friendship and wise counsel.

Keith Blevens and Valda Monroe, for your friendship, the single paradigm and everything else.

Chip and Jan Chipman, for your friendship and for speaking directly to who I really am.

Sháá Wasmund, for your friendship, mentorship and for asking me the *number one result* question all those years ago.

Deborah Banner, Jonny Bowden, Vanessa Pringle, Dzidek Sabat and Mandy Spray for your passion, genius and tireless support.

Nikki Owen, for your love, and for keeping the wheels on for all this time.

Tilly, Boo and all my family, my heart is filled with gratitude and love for you.

And finally, to Sydney Banks, for uncovering the principles behind clarity and sharing them with the world.

Further Explorations

These are the books I most frequently recommend to (and often purchase for) my clients, friends and family...

The Missing Link: Reflections on Philosophy and Spirit by Sydney Banks (Lone Pine Publishing, 1998)

Instant Motivation: The Surprising Truth Behind What Really Drives Top Performance by Chantal Burns (Pearson, 2014)

The Path of No Resistance: Why Overcoming Is Simpler Than You Think by Garret Kramer (Greenleaf Book Group, 2015)

Stillpower: Excellence with Ease in Sports and Life by Garret Kramer (Simon & Schuster, 2012)

Invisible Power: Insight Principles at Work by Ken Manning, Robin Charbit and Sandra Krot (Insight Principles, 2015)

The Inside-Out Revolution: The Only Thing You Need to Know to Change Your Life Forever by Michael Neill (Hay House, 2013)

The Space Within: Finding Your Way Back Home by Michael Neill (Hay House, 2016)

CLARITY: Clear Mind, Better Performance, Bigger Results by Jamie Smart (Wiley, 2013)

The Little Book of Clarity by Jamie Smart (Wiley, 2015)

You can find more educational materials, including audios, videos and distance learning programmes at...

www.JamieSmart.com

CLARITY® for Transformation Professionals

···

Jamie Smart is passionate about supporting transformation professionals (e.g. coaches, trainers, consultants, therapists, change-workers etc) in bringing the principles behind clarity into their work with clients, into their own practices and into their lives.

Are you passionate about making a difference? Jamie has a variety of programmes serving the growing community of transformation professionals who are leveraging the principles behind clarity in their work with clients and growing their practices. These include virtual courses, 1:1 coaching and the *Clarity Certification Programmes*.

All the programmes are oriented around the three essential transformations you need to share this understanding at a professional level: 1) *Grounding* – deepening your embodied understanding of these principles, 2) *Impact* – increasing your ability to share this understanding with others and 3) *Leverage* – discovering the keys to making your living 'from the inside-out' and taking your practice or business to the next level. These programmes are also popular with entrepreneurs, business owners and other leaders who want to bring an understanding of these principles into their work and their lives.

If you're a transformation professional and want to take things to a new level, here's what to do next:

1   Download the book **Your Exponential Practice Scorecard** to identify your sticking points, leverage points and quick wins for taking your grounding, impact and practice to a new level. It's a quick read with a powerful effect, and you can get it for free at *www.JamieSmart.com/scorecard*

2   Join the **Exponential Practice Professional Group** and connect with the growing community of like-minded transformation professionals who are passionate about exponentially increasing their grounding, impact and their livelihood. You can join for free at *www.JamieSmart.com/expo*

3   Subscribe to Your **Exponential Practice Podcast** for free at www.jamiesmart.com/yepp

You can find details of the Clarity Certification Programmes at...

www.JamieSmart.com/professional

CLARITY® for
Personal Results

Do you want to experience greater clarity and more meaningful results in specific aspects of your life? Experience shows that as you get a deeper understanding of the principles behind clarity, you'll start noticing the *inevitable results* of living more closely in alignment with the reality you're built for. Some of the results people typically experience include...

- An effortlessly clear mind more of the time, with less stress and more clarity

- Better relationships, with more love and connection

- Healthier choices and improved decision-making

- Greater sense of purpose and courage, with less struggle and strain

- An increased ability to create the results that matter to you and for you

Here's what to do next:

1 Discover your personal CLARITY® *Quotient* by answering 20 simple questions (multiple-choice). This quick and easy

questionnaire gives you a snapshot of your current state of mind, including a stress score and an engagement score. You can get yours for free at *www.jamiesmart.com/CQ*

2   Subscribe to the results podcast for free at *www.jamiesmart .com/resultspodcast.*

3   Take the *30-day RESULTS Challenge* and discover what's possible for you at *www.jamiesmart.com/challenge*

www.jamiesmart.com/challenge

CLARITY® for Fast-growing Businesses

....

Leading a fast-growing business presents unique challenges and big opportunities. But all too often, the thinking and actions that bring success at *one* level are the very things standing in the way of growing to the *next* level. Now add exponential technology, information overload and increasing disruption into the mix. When people look to you for clarity, confidence and certainty in the face of these challenges, it can sometimes seem like a tall order. Leading a successful organization can sometimes be isolating and even lonely when everyone else seems to be relying on you for the answers.

Your biggest leverage point for navigating times of volatility, complexity and uncertainty is your mindset. You need *less* on your mind, not *more* to think about. A clear mind opens the door to insight, innovation and high performance in your professional life. And as you increase your levels of clarity, you create the space for connection, fulfilment and peace of mind in your personal life.

The CLARITY 1:1 CEO Intensive is for business leaders who want to experience real and lasting transformation; a 'quantum shift' in your personal and professional life. You can get the full details and apply for a CEO Intensive at...

www.JamieSmart.com/CEO

CLARITY® for Large Organizations

....

Who's your most dangerous competitor? It's common sense to evaluate the threat they present. But all too often, *evaluation* slips into *preoccupation*. What have they got up their sleeves? What are they about to do that we don't know about? How badly could it hurt us?

Nobody does their best thinking when they're preoccupied. And when you're preoccupied, it always seems like you need more...

More thinking about what they're up to and how to beat them. More competitive analysis... more strategy... more incremental wins. *Hyatt* were so focused on one-upping *Marriott* and *Hilton* that by the time *Airbnb.com* was on their radar, the race was already over.

If the answer was 'more', you would already have it by now. But what if the answer *isn't* 'more'? What if the answer is 'less'?

Your most dangerous 'competitor' is contaminated thinking
You and your team already have the capacity to capitalize on the opportunities that lie ahead. As you *subtract* the compelling but unhelpful thinking that's been preoccupying you, you release the innate capacity for realization, intuition and innovation you need.

This is the basis for the kind of bold leaps that 'hit the ball where the competition isn't'.

To find out if your organization is a good fit for a *Clarity Consulting* project, visit:

www.ClarityConsulting.co.uk

The World Clarity Foundation

The *World Clarity Foundation* is a not-for-profit social enterprise created to relieve chronic psychological suffering globally, starting with specific communities. Our vision is for children to be born into a world where people have a foundational understanding that clarity is the mind's natural state and that innate psychological wellbeing exists within all of us.

The *Foundation* provides programmes, coaching, training and education based on the principles behind clarity of mind, psychological, social and emotional wellbeing.

Working with health and educational bodies, businesses and NGOs, our aim over the next few years is to build a network of like-minded individuals who can initiate self-starting, grassroots programmes. These will focus on combatting stress, anxiety, depression and addiction.

It is for these reasons that the Foundation is seeking to build committed communities of professionals and organizations that have social value at their heart.

To find out more and to see how you can get involved, please email info@worldclarity.com or visit

www.WorldClarity.com

About Jamie Smart

Jamie Smart is a number 1 bestselling author, coach and consultant. He is a renowned speaker, presenting regularly at major conferences worldwide. He shows individuals and organizations the unexpected keys to clarity; the ultimate leverage point for creating profound transformation and meaningful results.

Jamie's primary focus is in showing transformation professionals and business leaders how to bring the principles behind clarity into their work with clients, into their own businesses and into every aspect of their lives. In addition, he works with a handful of 1:1 coaching clients and leads selected corporate programmes.

Jamie's corporate clients range from an SME ranked as one of *The Sunday Times 100 Best Small Companies to Work For* to a Fortune 500 business designated by Ethisphere as one of the *World's Most Ethical Companies*. He has appeared on Sky TV and on the BBC, as well as in numerous publications including *The Times, The Daily Telegraph, The Huffington Post* and *Psychologies Magazine*. As well as *RESULTS: Think Less, Achieve More,* he is also the author of the books *CLARITY: Clear Mind, Better Performance, Bigger Results* and *The Little Book of Clarity*.

Jamie lives in the UK. When he's not working, he loves spending time with his daughters, travelling, walking, drinking coffee and exploring.

You can find full contact details at www.JamieSmart.com/contact. You can read Jamie's blog at www.JamieSmart.com, connect with him on Facebook at www.Facebook.com/jamiesmartltd, on Snapchat at @jsmart999 and on Twitter at @Jamie_Smart_

www.JamieSmart.com

Index